I0901191

TO:

FROM:

DATE:

It's hard to think of a more timely message than Dave Smith's invitation to whole-life whole-person wellbeing. This is not just some kind of buzz word; it's a profoundly biblical concept of shalom affecting every single area of life. Dave Smith is the kind of leader who practices what he preaches and this message has been outworked in the lives of thousands already. I'm particularly glad that he has covered such a wide range of aspects of wellbeing—from mental health to finances and vocation. This is a brilliant and timely resource.
Pete Greig, 24-7 Prayer International and Emmaus Rd Church

In the times that we are living in, the topic of wellbeing has never been more relevant or important. In this brilliant book, Dave Smith encourages us to approach wellbeing holistically, exploring how we can each grow in physical, emotional, spiritual, relational, financial, and vocational health. Using biblical insights, psychological and medical perspectives, as well as lessons from his own personal story, Dave offers bite-sized daily meditations and practical next-steps suggestions to help us on our journey of increasing wellbeing. As someone who has been through my own struggles with wellbeing, I can't recommend this timely book enough.
Simon Thomas

The Wellbeing Journey has a prophetic edge in this season. Jesus is "the Prince of Wholeness" as The Message version translates Isaiah 9:6. Following the 2020 COVID-19 pandemic, local churches are in a unique place to lead communities on this journey to physical, mental, and spiritual wellbeing as they offer this practical guide.
Roy Crowne, HOPE Together's Executive Director

Dave Smith is one of the most gifted Christian leaders in the UK today and I am delighted that he has produced this exciting new book to help all of us grow in wellbeing.
Nicky Gumbel, Vicar of HTB and pioneer of Alpha

This is so timely to produce a series for the church to walk through and I highly recommend it. The book is practical and insightful—something for every day. It covers all aspects of wellbeing including financial, physical, and spiritual wellbeing—it's a journey. I strongly endorse this.
Natalie Andrews, National Sport and Wellbeing Project Lead

Wellbeing is the subject of the moment and Dave Smith's book expertly tackles it from God's perspective. Is God genuinely interested in our wellbeing or are we just following the cultural tide? Could we flourish in life if we changed some of our personal habits? What practical steps do we need to take for greater wellbeing? You'll find the answers in the pages of this book.
Dr. Rachel Jordan-Wolf, Assistant Director HOPE Together

There could never be a better time for a book on wellbeing. As the world grapples with the impact of the COVID-19 pandemic, months of prolonged isolation during lockdown have put a strain on mental health and wellbeing, relationships, and finances. There has been loss of life, often under difficult circumstances, and the usual grieving process has been affected by restrictions to prevent the spread of the virus.

This timely book is such a rich resource for anyone who desires to find that equilibrium of physical, mental, and social wellbeing. While this area is awash with self-help books, what sets this book apart is that it clearly points us to God as the source of our wellbeing. References to Dave's personal journey add authenticity to the book and its simple prose makes it easy reading. This book is certainly a must-read in this new normal and I wholeheartedly recommend it.
Agu Irukwu, Senior Pastor Jesus House for All Nations. Chair Executive Council Redeemed Christian Church of God UK

Dave Smith has learned the lessons of wellbeing the hard way, by asking tough personal questions and finding answers that can help us all. To my mind, this is one of the best wellbeing resources available to Christians. It distills biblical, psychological, and medical expertise into bite-sized meditations covering all aspects of wellbeing, and most importantly, offers practical steps we can all take towards living life to the full. This book is a repository of wisdom and a gift to the church. It isn't even out yet and I've been recommending it furiously.
Dr. Roger Bretherton, Clinical Psychologist and Associate Professor in Psychology, University of Lincoln (UK)

The paradox of our world today is that we have more information, knowledge, amenities, and opportunities than ever before, and yet we feel depleted, exhausted, and emptier than ever before, and our wellbeing is what is at stake. With practical wisdom and biblical truth, David Smith encapsulates Jesus' heart for us by showing how we can be "made whole," not just for a moment in life but throughout the seasons of life.
Pastor Tope Koleoso, Jubilee Church London

Never has the issue of wellbeing seemed so pertinent. Dave Smith's new book, resulting from years of "walking the walk" himself, is pleasing in every way. It is biblically-based, carefully considered, practically presented, and ... timely! Dave addresses so many aspects of our lives, be they physical or emotional, financial or spiritual, vocational or relational. And to have woven them into a single tapestry, as in this wonderful book, is skillful indeed.
Eleanor Mumford, Vineyard Churches

A 50-DAY GUIDE

LIVE WELL

GOD'S PLAN FOR YOUR WELLBEING

DAVE SMITH

Christian Art PUBLISHERS

Visit Christian Art Gifts, Inc., at www.christianartgifts.com.

Live Well: God's Plan for Your Wellbeing

Previously published by CWR (United Kingdom) under the title *God's Plan for Your Wellbeing: 50-Day Guide*. Copyright © 2020. Reformatted 2025 as a gift edition by Christian Art Publishers, Inc.

© 2020 by Dave Smith. All rights reserved.

Gift edition published by Christian Art Gifts, Inc., Bloomingdale, IL, USA in partnership with Kobus Johnsen of Johnsen, Inc.

First edition 2025.

Designed by Christian Art Gifts, Inc.

Cover and interior images used under license from Shutterstock.com.

Unless otherwise indicated, Scripture references are taken from the Holy Bible, New International Version® Copyright © 1979, 1984, 2011 by Biblica, Inc.® Used by permission. All rights reserved worldwide.

Scripture quotations marked AMP are taken from the Amplified Bible. Copyright © 2015 by The Lockman Foundation, La Habra, CA 90631. All rights reserved.

Scripture marked BSB are taken from The Holy Bible, Berean Study Bible, BSB Copyright ©2016, 2018 by Bible Hub. All rights reserved.

Scripture quotations marked ESV are taken from the Holy Bible, English Standard Version®. Copyright © 2001 by Crossway, a publishing ministry of Good News Publishers. All rights reserved.

Scripture marked NASB are taken from New American Standard Bible. Copyright © 1960, 1962, 1963, 1968, 1971, 1972, 1973, 1975, 1977, 1995 by The Lockman Foundation. All rights reserved.

Scripture quotations marked NKJV are taken from the New King James Version®. Copyright © 1982 by Thomas Nelson. Used by permission. All rights reserved.

Scripture quotations marked NLT are taken from The Holy Bible, New Living Translation, copyright © 1996, 2004, 2015 by Tyndale House Foundation. Used by permission of Tyndale House Publishers, Inc., Carol Stream, Illinois 60188. All rights reserved.

Scripture quotations marked *The Message* are taken from THE MESSAGE, copyright © 1993, 2002, 2018 by Eugene H. Peterson. Used by permission of NavPress. All rights reserved. Represented by Tyndale House Publishers, Inc.

Scripture quotations marked NRSV are from the New Revised Standard Version Bible, copyright © 1989 the Division of Christian Education of the National Council of the Churches of Christ in the United States of America. Used by permission. All rights reserved.

© All rights reserved. No part of this book may be reproduced in any form without permission in writing from the publisher, except in the case of brief quotations embodied in critical articles or reviews.

Most Christian Art titles may be purchased at bulk discounts by churches, nonprofits, and corporations. For more information, please email SpecialMarkets@cagifts.com.

ISBN 978-1-63952-904-9

Printed in China.

30 29 28 27 26 25
10 9 8 7 6 5 4 3 2 1

I want to say a special thanks to a number of people: to Dr. Roger Bretherton for his valuable, professional insights, especially on emotional health; to Dr. Tom Campion and Larry Warner, for their personal help on my wellbeing journey and for their encouragement in this project; to Jeff Lucas for his ongoing friendship, advice and encouragement; to Roy Crowne and Rachel Jordan-Wolf for their partnership and comments; to J. John for his insight and feedback; to Dr. Andrew Ollerton for his biblical perspectives and to Dr. Nkiru Oluwatosin for her medical insights; and to members of my family, friends, and KingsGate team—Simon Deeks, Chris and Annabel Sharman, Jasmine Allen, Matt Cernik, Galia Ben-Israel, Tom Webster, Emily Wimborne, and Alexandra Cutteridge—who have all provided valuable input along the way.

A particular thanks to my wife Karen for her amazing love, faithfulness, and support during 35 years of marriage, and for her detailed feedback during the writing process. Finally, a big thanks to all at KingsGate Church. It's great to be on this wellbeing journey together!

Contents

Introduction

A JOURNEY TO LIVE WELL

I am so excited that you have decided to pick up this book! From a personal perspective, I know how much the lessons I am going to be sharing have changed, and are still changing, my life today.

My story in a nutshell is this: I grew up in a secure home, went completely off the rails in my teens, became a Christian in college, and then immediately began to experience a radical transformation. But a few years ago, nearly 35 years after my first decision to follow Jesus, I began a new journey of transformation—an attempt to live well physically, emotionally, spiritually, relationally, financially, and vocationally. I called it my "journey to wellbeing." As I have begun to share my experience and the things I've learned more widely, I've been very encouraged by how helpful others have found them. I trust that these lessons will be beneficial to you, too.

On a broader level, wellbeing is both a timely and a timeless issue. As I developed this material, I dug into the concept and realized it is of prime concern in our society right now. For example, in a conversation with a local government official in late September 2019, she declared that, from her perspective, wellbeing was "the key issue." As I write, it is the summer of 2020, and the whole world has been rocked by the coronavirus pandemic. It seems as if the hugely disruptive impact of this crisis has only made the subject of wellbeing in our lives more important than ever.

So, whether you consider yourself a person of faith or not, whether you are struggling to thrive in an area of your life or just want to be healthier overall, I hope that this book will be of great benefit to you.

To begin our shared journey to live well, let's start with a definition of the word that sums up our goal: wellbeing. The Oxford English Dictionary defines it as "the state of being comfortable, healthy, and happy." *Psychology Today* goes along with this but also includes "having good mental health, high life satisfaction, and a sense of meaning or purpose. More generally, wellbeing is just feeling well."[1]

Clearly, many in our society are consistently not feeling well. In a 2023 survey conducted by the American Psychological Association,[2] 26% of U.S. adults reported that on most days their stress is completely overwhelming; 22% said they are so stressed they feel numb; and 20% described being so stressed most days that they can't function. Sadly, such pressures are also impacting children and young people, with research indicating that over 75% of mental health problems occur before the age of 25.[3] The continuing impact of COVID-19 is only making this situation significantly worse; not least because of the significant restrictions on in-person connections. While connecting digitally has many benefits, too much screen time can be exhausting. Moreover, through social media, we can, at a single touch, view the highlight reel of other people's seemingly great lives—and if we're not secure, we can easily descend into a negative spiral of comparison.

The good news, though, is that you and I can take active steps to live well—to achieve wellbeing—by becoming more aware of how we are doing in various areas of our lives and taking appropriate action to see improvement. Let me use the analogy of a car: regularly checking the different dials on the dashboard and acting accordingly is vital to ensuring optimum performance on the one hand and avoiding permanent damage on the other! A core part of this 50-day guide is thinking of our lives as having six different but interrelated "tanks," each having a "dial" on our "dashboard." These six key areas are physical, emotional, spiritual, relational, financial, and vocational. Each is vital, and all are interrelated, meaning that an increase or decrease in how much we're thriving in any

one of those areas is likely to have an impact on one, or all, of the others.

Since each of these areas of our lives is so important, we are going to be spending a few days on each. For now, why not imagine enjoying:

- Higher levels of physical energy and health
- An increase in emotional freedom and peace
- A heightened sense of spiritual satisfaction in the deepest part of you
- Deeper relational connection and harmony with others
- Greater financial margin and peace, enabling you to live a life of generosity
- A stronger sense of vocational motivation and creativity aligned with your purpose and calling

Throughout the coming weeks, you will have regular opportunities for self-assessment so that you can more accurately diagnose where you are, rather than having a general feeling of something being "not quite right." You may simply be seeking an increased sense of thriving in all areas of your life, or you may be facing acute stress, depression, or burnout. The reality is that none of us has achieved complete wellbeing; we're all on a journey of trying to live well.

Speaking of journeys, my wife Karen and I went away to a friend's lodge in a National Park area called Exmoor to celebrate our thirty-fourth wedding anniversary. It was our second visit—the previous year we had gone for a walk to a place called Dunkery Beacon, the highest peak on Exmoor, only to get lost and have to turn back. So, we thought we'd try again, and for a second year running, we got lost and had to turn back! Not to be daunted, we got in the car, put on our GPS, took a different route, parked, and managed the 30-minute walk to the top, to be rewarded with stunning 360-degree views.

Our journeys of trying to live well can be a bit like this: it's easy to get lost on the way and might take perseverance, but when we get there, it all feels so worthwhile! With that in mind, at the outset, I want to share three things we need to do if we are to move toward thriving in all areas of our lives. First, we need to ...

1. Follow the best directions.

That was our first problem on our Exmoor journey: we didn't have proper directions. We didn't have a paper map because there was no printer, and we didn't have a digital map because 4G wasn't working for my phone. So we set out in what I thought was the right direction, following the signs as best as we could, not helped by the fact that, as we later discovered, one of the signs was actually pointing in the wrong direction!

When it comes to living well, it's even more critical that we find and follow the best possible directions. The good news is that there are more resources than ever before, including 120 million videos on YouTube and many best-selling books focusing on specific areas of wellbeing. The not-so-great news is that there is so much material that it can be overwhelming and difficult to decide which sources are the most helpful and trustworthy.

Fortunately, as you're going to see throughout this 50-day guide, we have one go-to source—like a superb map—which gives the best, most accurate, and comprehensive directions for living well in all areas of our lives: the Bible. The Bible is a collection of sacred texts or scriptures, comprising 66 volumes, and structured into two main sections, Old Testament and New Testament. Over 1,900 years since the last book of the Bible was penned, it continues to be the world's bestseller year after year. It's influenced our calendars, dividing history into before and after the arrival of its central character, Jesus Christ. The Bible has also shaped our culture, inspiring great literary classics, songs, and works of art. It's been instrumental in movements and revolutions such as the abolition of slavery, the development of medicine and hospitals, and is the source of inspiration for many of our laws. Great figures have long recognized its huge impact. For example:

> *"It is impossible to rightly govern the world without God and the Bible."*
> (George Washington)

> *"The Bible is no mere book, but a living Creature, with a power that conquers all that oppose it."*
> (Napoleon)

What Napoleon is implying here is that the Bible is more than just a best-selling, highly influential collection of writings. Rather, as the Bible itself claims, it is inspired by God (2 Timothy 3:16), meaning that God is the ultimate author, inspiring the different human authors as they spoke and wrote. Hence, the Bible acts not like a static map, but more like Google Maps, able to locate us where we are and help point us in the right direction. In the words of the psalmist, we can begin to discover the truth that: "Your word [the Bible] is a lamp for my feet, a light on my path" (Psalm 119:105).

Even if you are not a Christian, or you are not sure about the divine inspiration of Scripture, you can be confident that the Bible provides a wealth of insight on how to live well. If you don't have a copy of the Bible, you can read it on an App called YouVersion (www.youversion.com). I personally came to accept the Bible as God's Word shortly after I became a Christian. Even though I love to study and read lots of books, including materials on wellbeing, I have never come across anything like the Bible. Over many years, its insights have given me a broad overview of who God is and of His plan for how life should be lived. Moreover, there have been countless times when I have sensed God speaking to me through the Bible, nudging me to act in ways that have indeed improved my life and the lives of those around me.

While the word "wellbeing" doesn't appear in many English translations of the Bible, there's a hugely important Hebrew word that perfectly expresses God's passion and plan for our thriving: ***shalom***. Whereas ***shalom*** is normally translated into English as "peace"—primarily associated with an absence of conflict or one's inner serenity—true *shalom* is a much richer word encompassing wholeness, health, and harmony. *Shalom* means taking joy in and being rightly related to God, to others, to oneself, and to the created world. In summary, it is about experiencing complete wellbeing in every area of life. The word *shalom* appears over 250 times in the Old Testament, and the Greek equivalent, *eirene* (peace) appears in the New Testament over 90 times. The significant usage of these "peace" words highlights God's wonderful plan for human flourishing.

As well as following the best directions, the second thing we need to do as we embark on our journey to live well is to ...

2. Seek expert guidance.

When you go on a journey, it's great to have an accurate digital map, but it's even better to also have someone with you who knows the way. When I mentioned to our friend that we had gotten lost for a second time on our walk to Dunkery Beacon, he said, "Oh, when our daughter Emma stays here, she runs it every morning!" Part of me thought, *Well, that didn't help us.* What we needed was for Emma to actually accompany us on the journey. Since she has been there many times before and fully knows the way, she would have provided a fail-safe way for us to take the right path.

A similar principle applies to our journey: there's nothing like having a person who is an expert in a particular area, and who knows us so well that they can customize a plan and give advice that exactly fits where we're at. The reality is that most of us probably don't have the time or the resources to get personalized, specialist help in every area of our lives. However, there is someone who knows more about your physical wellness than the best physical trainer, nutritionist, sleep expert, or doctor. He knows more about your emotional wellness than the best psychologist or counselor. He knows more about your spiritual wellness than the best guru, religious leader, or philosopher. He knows more about your relational wellness than the best relational coach or marriage counselor. He knows more about your financial wellness than the best financial planner you could possibly find. He knows more about your vocational wellness than the best career advisor. I'm talking about God Himself.

It is not just that God shows us how to find wellbeing; He Himself is our wellbeing. In the culture of the Bible, where names meant a lot more than they do in Western culture today, it's highly significant that one of the names of God is Yahweh-Shalom, translated as "The LORD Is Peace [wellbeing]" (Judges 6:24). Moreover, if we take a very brief overview of the Bible's big story, we can see the following stages in God's plan for and active involvement in our wellbeing.

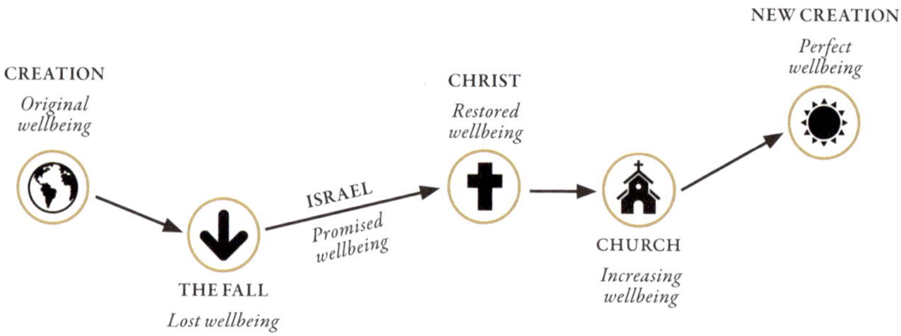

- **Original wellbeing:** In the first two chapters of the book of Genesis, there's a beautiful picture of the first human beings (called Adam and Eve), made in the image of God, designed for relationship with God and one another, enjoying wellbeing in the blissful setting of the Garden of Eden with their every need supplied—physically, emotionally, spiritually, relationally, materially, and vocationally. Imagine living in complete harmony and tranquility with every need met and without worry or fear!

- **Lost wellbeing:** Tragically, humans decided to turn their backs on God, thereby losing peace with God, with each other, and with their world. Their relationships became strained, their work became hard, and suffering and death entered the earth (see Genesis 3; Romans 5:12).

- **Promised wellbeing:** Thankfully, God decided to begin again, making a covenant with a man called Abram and his descendants, so they could enjoy a measure of wellbeing as they kept their part of the covenant to believe and walk in God's ways (see Genesis 12–15). There were brief seasons when the people of God enjoyed this *shalom*, but these were only a foretaste of the fullness of wellbeing that was promised when the Savior would come (see Micah 4:4; Isaiah 9:6–7).

- **Restored wellbeing:** This promise of peace began to be gloriously fulfilled when God sent His Son, Jesus Christ, from heaven. During His earthly ministry, Jesus—the only perfect human being who ever lived—went around doing good and bringing wellbeing to all who were oppressed (see Acts 10:38). Then He died on the cross, paying the price for us to enjoy true peace with God and wellbeing in every part of our lives, before rising triumphantly from the grave, giving us the power to be born again and become children of God (see John 1:12).

- **Increasing wellbeing:** All those who now follow Jesus and receive the Holy Spirit are invited to enjoy increasing wellbeing from the inside out.

- **Perfect wellbeing:** This will be available only when Jesus comes back to restore all things upon His return. In the last two chapters of the Bible, we see a beautiful picture of God dwelling with people, and of a restored and perfect wellbeing throughout the whole new heavens and new earth, when "He'll wipe every tear from their eyes. Death is gone for good—tears gone, crying gone, pain gone. ... [God will say], 'Look! I'm making everything new'" (Revelation 21:4–5 *The Message*).

So, that leaves us with the possibility of enjoying increasing wellbeing through Jesus now and the assurance of enjoying perfect wellbeing at His return!

This is more than something that is just broadly true for humanity in general. It's true for us personally since God is someone who knows us better than we know ourselves and has a plan for our lives. You may not consider yourself "religious" or "a person of faith," let alone a full-fledged Christian. However, given that one of the key areas of our wellness is "spiritual" (and as we shall see, it is central to our overall thriving), I would encourage you to be open-minded as you go on this journey.

The third thing that will help you on your journey is to make a decision to ...

3. Travel with others.

I'm so glad that Karen and I were together on our Exmoor journey, especially after we'd made it through a brief marital argument that went something like this: "No, it's this way." "No, it's this way ..." Followed by, "I'm not going any further up that hill!" (I'll leave you to imagine who said that!) I'm particularly glad that we were together when the soles of both Karen's walking shoes came off within half an hour of each other. I'm so glad that we could encourage one another to keep going, and I'm so glad that when we finally got to the top, we could celebrate a special wedding anniversary as we took in the stunning views together.

The fact is that what was true for a physical journey is even more the case when it comes to the journey of life. Put simply, we weren't designed to do life alone. Ecclesiastes 4:9–12, a well-known passage of the Bible, says it this way:

> *"Two are better than one, because they have a good return for their labor: If either of them falls down, one can help the other up. But pity anyone who falls and has no one to help them up. Also, if two lie down together, they will keep warm. But how can one keep warm alone? Though one may be overpowered, two can defend themselves. A cord of three strands is not quickly broken."*

Often quoted at weddings, this text emphasizes the importance and power of close, healthy human relationships—something that we'll be exploring in more detail when we look at how to live well relationally. Personally, I've found that throughout my attempts to live well (especially in the last three or four years), having other close, wise, and trusted people has been absolutely critical. In fact, I would say I wouldn't have gotten where I am right now without these significant "others." So I really encourage you that although this book is something you can go through by yourself, if you can find a friend you can journey with or a wellness group that you can participate in, your growth will be greatly enhanced.

BIBLICAL BACKGROUND TO THE STORY OF ELIJAH

To help us explore God's plan for how to live well, we'll be looking at the story of an Old Testament prophet, Elijah. He's a great example of someone who seemed to be strong and doing well, and yet had a sudden and complete burnout, before being lovingly restored by the Lord.

At first glance, this seems surprising—Elijah is a kind of Old Testament superhero, who spoke and acted in a miraculous way before being transported to heaven without experiencing physical death. But that's why his complete collapse is all the more remarkable. The New Testament writer James brings out this contrast. While upholding Elijah as an exemplary man of great faith and prayer, James points out that, nevertheless, "Elijah was a man just like us" (James 5:17 BSB), or as another translation puts it, he was "as human as we are" (NLT). Although Elijah lived in a very different time and context to ours, there are many lessons from his life for us today. So, while this book is not a study of the life of Elijah but rather a practical guide to God's plan for our wellbeing, we will glean from Elijah's story to help illustrate the themes of replenishment and wellness. His story is instructive, although it doesn't illustrate every point I want to make—and where that is the case, I won't try to make the link! Hence, I will also be drawing from wider biblical material,[4] as well as that of modern-day psychological studies.

Before we focus on specific incidents from Elijah's life, it would be helpful to take a few minutes to get a wide-angle view of the whole story, which you can find in the Bible from 1 Kings 17 through 2 Kings 2. It would be useful if you could take a few minutes to read through 1 Kings 17–19, especially chapter 19, where the themes of wellbeing, burnout, and replenishment are most evident.

Here are a few background facts and a simple summary of the biblical narrative to guide you in your reading.

Elijah was born around 2,900 years ago in a place called Tishbe, in Gilead (thought by historians to be modern-day Jordan). For many years, the nation of Israel had been experiencing serious spiritual and moral decay. The golden era of kings David and Solomon was well and truly a thing of the past. Since then, six wicked kings had reigned in just 58 years. Now the seventh king, Ahab, was on the throne (from 874 BC) and he was worse than the rest. He married Jezebel, a princess fanatically devoted to Baal worship and its toxic mix of occult power, sexual rituals, and child sacrifice. Jezebel began killing the prophets of God and raising up her own prophets to Baal and the goddess Asherah.

It was against this dark backdrop that the prophet Elijah dramatically appeared on the scene, pronouncing judgment on the king and the nation. Here's a brief timeline of the story:

— ELIJAH'S EARLY MINISTRY —

(1 Kings 17—18)

- **Drought:** Elijah tells Ahab there will be no rain for the next few years (17:1).
- **Supernatural provision:** God tells Elijah to hide in the Kerith Ravine, where he will be fed by ravens (17:2–6).
- **More miraculous provision:** The Lord commands Elijah to travel to a widow's house in Zarephath. Through a miracle of food multiplication, Elijah, the widow, and her son are all provided for (17:9–16).
- **Resurrection:** The son suddenly dies. Elijah prays and God raises him from the dead (17:17–24).
- **Confrontation:** God tells Elijah to present himself to Ahab (18:1).
- **Secret agent:** Obadiah, a devout believer in the Lord, meets Elijah. Ahab goes with Obadiah to meet Elijah (18:7, 16).
- **Victory:** Elijah invites God to bring down fire, thus triumphing over the false prophets (18:19–39). Elijah has the prophets of Baal killed (18:40).
- **The drought ends:** Elijah prays and summons rain (18:42–45).
- **Power:** The Spirit of the Lord comes upon Elijah and he outruns the king's chariot (18:46).

— ELIJAH'S COLLAPSE AND RESTORATION —

(1 Kings 19:1–18)

- **Panic:** Elijah flees in fear from Jezebel and lies down in the desert to die (19:1–5).
- **Replenishment:** An angel of the Lord revives and feeds him (19:5–7).
- **Pilgrimage:** Elijah goes on a 40-day journey to Mount Horeb (19:8–9).
- **Encounter:** Elijah meets with the Lord, who speaks to him in a gentle whisper (19:9–14).
- **Recommissioning:** God tells Elijah to go back and anoint two new kings and to call a young man, Elisha, to succeed him as prophet (19:15–17).

— ELIJAH'S LATER YEARS —

(1 Kings 19:19 — 2 Kings 2:11)

- **Successor:** Elijah anoints Elisha as prophet; Elisha leaves his home and work to become Elijah's servant (19:19–21).
- **Prophesying:** Elijah prophesies the death of Ahab and Jezebel (21:17–19, 23). Ahab dies as the Lord had told Elijah (22:34–35).
- **King Ahaziah:** Ahaziah becomes King of Israel (22:51). Elijah sends him a message that he will die in bed (2 Kings 1:4). Ahaziah sends troops to Elijah. Elijah goes to Ahaziah (1:9–15).
- **King Joram:** Ahaziah dies, as God said he would, and Joram becomes King of Israel (1:17).
- **A glorious ending:** The Lord takes Elijah to heaven in a chariot of fire and Elisha succeeds him as prophet (2:11).

HOW TO GET THE MOST OUT OF THIS GUIDE

Let me encourage you to start this 50-day journey with a sense of confidence that God wants to help you live well in every area of your life.

Before we look at some foundational principles for developing the right mindset, why not prepare for the rest of the journey by pausing for a few moments to look at each of the six dials on your life dashboard—physical, emotional, spiritual, relational, financial, and vocational. Then start with a simple self-assessment, thinking about whether those dials are green (healthy and full), yellow (needing attention), or red (unhealthy or near empty). Finish by taking a moment to ask God to replenish you and help you establish new habits in all these areas, especially in the ones where you feel most depleted.

Here are a few tips to help you get the most out of your reading over the next 50 days.

Read and Record

The reading material is deliberately short so that it's easy to fit into a busy schedule. I encourage you to try to find a fixed time every day that works for you and then read the content slowly to allow yourself to properly digest it. You may want to jot down and highlight things that particularly stand out to you.

Reflect and Respond

Each day has a "reflect and respond" section. This is designed to help you take time to reflect on any key points for that day and consider whether there are any practical steps you might want to take further. It can be helpful to write them down and then go back to them at the end of the week or turn them into an action point.

Major on Holistic Activities

At the end of the 50 days, you will have identified a few key areas that you want to develop further. Try to put these in prioritized order and consider if there's one key activity that will have a significant impact on many areas of your life. As a personal example (which I share later), going on walks is probably my number-one holistic tank-filling exercise. It has the physical benefits of helping me to stay fit and fresh and encourages me to eat more healthily and to sleep better. But it also gives me time to think and process my feelings, and so has a huge impact on my emotional and spiritual health as well. Very often this then overflows into helping me relationally and vocationally, too! Hopefully, you'll be able to discover the one or two key holistic activities that best suit you.

Before we look at this whole subject in more detail, if you're already a follower of Jesus, let me encourage you to take time to celebrate and thank God for His master plan for your wellbeing and invite His Spirit to help you grow in the freedom and blessing that has already been won for you. If you are not a Christian or don't believe in God, then I'm especially pleased that you've started this journey of exploration. If at any point you want to begin a close, personal relationship with Him, then you can pray the prayer at the back.

No matter how you are setting out, let's begin with these words of Jesus:

> *"Come to me. Get away with me and you'll recover your life. I'll show you how to take a real rest. Walk with me and work with me—watch how I do it. Learn the unforced rhythms of grace. ... Keep company with me and you'll learn to live freely and lightly."*
>
> *(Matthew 11:28–30 The Message)*

A MINDSET TO LIVE WELL

DAY 1

Peace of mind

"We demolish arguments and every pretension that sets itself up against the knowledge of God, and we take captive every thought to make it obedient to Christ."

2 CORINTHIANS 10:5

One of the most defining occasions of my life was a visit to 10 Downing Street.

I had been invited along with my wife, Karen, and a number of other church leaders, to hear from the Prime Minister. However, I found myself so engrossed in conversation with one of my pastor friends, that I didn't even notice that the Prime Minister had entered the room. This friend was sharing how he and his wife had been navigating a life-changing and potentially very stressful situation by receiving significant help from both a spiritual director and a Christian psychologist. Although I wasn't in a crisis season, I was able to see that prevention is better than cure, so I asked my friend to help me get in touch with both of them. In ways that I hadn't anticipated, the spiritual director has helped me to grow to a deeper level in my spirituality and the psychologist has enabled me to develop healthier ways of thinking and "perspectives" (his favorite word!), which in turn has had a hugely positive impact on my emotional wellbeing.

As we begin this 50-day guide, I want to start by focusing on the issue of our perspectives by looking at how we can develop the right mindset to live well. It is so important that we start here because the way we think impacts every part of our lives. To use a horticultural image: if we want the fruits of thriving—physically, emotionally, spiritually, relationally, financially, and vocationally—we need to attend to the roots—in this case, our thinking. In the words of Selwyn Hughes, founder of Crusade for World Revival: "To win the battle of the mind is to win in one of the greatest areas of life. ... It is said that no real change can take place until a person's thinking is changed."[1]

This link between a healthy mindset and our overall thriving can be medically verified. One of the doctors in our local church recently wrote to me about the strong link between our mental state and the symptoms of stress, such as headaches, muscle tension, dizziness, sleep problems, tiredness, irritability, and feeling overwhelmed, anxious, or fearful. She said, "From my personal experience, my clinical practice, and ongoing current research in neuroscience, I have come to understand that the link between mental stress and the physical body cannot be overemphasized." Then, drawing on her own medical background and the Bible, she gave "8 Tips on How to Live a Stress-Free Life," many of which are related to our thoughts and our mindset:

1. **Use mindfulness and meditation.** These practices are frequently recommended for increased mental wellbeing. Christian mindfulness is becoming aware of the presence of God, and Christian meditation focuses on the Word of God (see Joshua 1:8). Together they produce wonderful benefits: "You will keep in perfect peace ['complete wellbeing,' literally 'shalom, shalom'] those whose minds are steadfast, because they trust in you" (Isaiah 26:3 AMP).
2. **Take control of your thoughts.** The U.S. National Institute of Mental Health (NIMH) website highlights the importance of this, suggesting: "Identify and challenge your negative and unhelpful thoughts."[2] The Bible calls us to "take captive every thought to make it obedient to Christ" (2 Corinthians 10:5).
3. **Develop the habit of casting your cares.** The Bible encourages "casting all your cares [all your anxieties, all your worries, and all your concerns, once and for all] on Him, for He cares about you [with deepest affection, and watches over you very carefully]" (1 Peter 5:7 AMP).

4. **Connect with people, help people.** Science has shown that as we do this, our neural networks form better. The Bible tells us we are to live a life of love (see 1 Corinthians 13).
5. **Do things you enjoy.** The NIMH advice to "schedule regular time for healthy activities you enjoy" confirms the biblical picture of the Creator God who "provides us with everything for our enjoyment" (1 Timothy 6:17).
6. **Be goal oriented.** Again, the NIMH advises you to set goals and priorities. The Bible talks about the importance of vision (see Proverbs 29:18) and has an underlying theme of the need for us to live with true purpose (which we'll address later in this book).
7. **Be thankful.** Research shows the people who are most grateful are generally more satisfied and less stressed. The Bible encourages us to give thanks in all things (see Colossians 3:16–17 and Day 19).
8. **Live loved.** The general term for this is self-love. The Bible tells us that we will only truly know we're loved when we know we're the beloved of God (see Ephesians 5:1–2 and Days 2 and 17).

What's encouraging about this list is that they are all things that are medically recommended, biblically based, and practically accessible.

REFLECT & RESPOND

Review the "8 Tips on How to Live a Stress-Free Life" and highlight which tips seem most pertinent to you. Pick the top one and ask God to begin to help you implement this in your life over these next 50 days and beyond!

DAY 2

"See what great love the Father has lavished on us, that we should be called children of God! And that is what we are!"

1 JOHN 3:1

Identity

For the next few days, I want to focus on perspectives that are of foundational importance in developing a mindset to live well. They are:

- Knowing who you really are (Days 2–3)
- Knowing where you're really at (Days 4–6)
- Knowing that you can really change (Day 7)

Today, I want to start with the first perspective, which concerns the crucial issue of knowing who we really are—that is, knowing our true identity.

Who Do You Think You Are? is more than the title of a long-running BBC series on family history. It is a key life question for all of us. How we answer that question and what we think about ourselves will have a huge bearing on how we live. For example, whether you and I think of ourselves as worthy and loved or unworthy and unlovable, will massively impact our sense of wellbeing and how we interact with others.

However, it's possible to have a sense of identity and lose it. It reminds me of the young lion cub Simba in Disney's *The Lion King*. The turning point of the story is when Simba, having forgotten his identity as the son of the king, has a vision of his father, Mufasa, appearing to him. Simba's revelation comes through Mufasa's unforgettable words: "Simba, remember who you are ... you are my son ... remember who you are."[3]

For us, the problem is that we can often struggle with confusion over our identity because we look for it in all the wrong places. Sometimes we can define ourselves by looking at and comparing ourselves to other people (not helped, as we said in the Introduction, by the mental bombardment of seeing other people's "successes" on social media). Other times, we can find ourselves simply looking at or within ourselves, thinking about the past, our present circumstances, or our uncertain future. Each of these can lead to an inaccurate view of who we are. The big-picture message of the Bible is that true identity comes not from within ourselves, or by comparing ourselves with others, but from an ever-growing relationship with the loving God who made us and who alone can satisfy our deepest needs.

This issue of identity was pivotal to the story of the main character of this guide, the Old Testament prophet Elijah. He is a great example of someone who started out well until he suddenly burned out, before being lovingly restored by God.

Although Elijah was born over 900 years before Jesus, his clear sense of identity as a servant of God was vital to the strength of his early ministry years. First, in a culture where names had huge significance, he was named "Eli-yah," which meant "The LORD is my God." The very first words we hear him say underline the fact that he had a strong sense of his God-given identity, self-worth, and significance: "As the LORD, the God of Israel, lives, before whom I stand ..." (1 Kings 17:1 ESV). Here was a man who clearly knew that he was called by God, and who had a strong relationship with God. But by the time of his burnout, he seems to have lost all sense of his true God-given identity and confidence, saying: "I have had enough, LORD. ... Take my life; *I am no better than my ancestors*" (1 Kings 19:4–5, my italics). We don't know anything about his ancestors, but he seems to have forgotten that he was different from them, that he was Eli-yah, one set apart to know and serve the real God.

So, what about us? The great news is that we have the potential for a far stronger sense of identity and self-worth than even the mighty Elijah. Because Jesus Christ, the

Son of God, came from heaven to earth, died on a cross for our sins, and is alive and seated again at the Father's right hand, we can enjoy an identity like no other. Through Christ and the presence of the Holy Spirit, we can become children of God and receive a new identity as those who are forgiven, adopted, and loved by God.

It's possible to be a Christian and not fully know who we really are in Christ—or, like Elijah, forget who we really are. I've discovered over the years that the truth of my identity in Christ is something that I need to return to again and again.[4] As I'll share later, one of the main ways that I've experienced greater freedom from drivenness and a fear of failure has been to regularly remind myself that in Christ I am deeply loved by God. Knowing who I really am then radically changes how I live. It highlights that, for all of us, knowing our true identity is key to developing a mindset that allows us to live well.

REFLECT & RESPOND

Do you struggle with either a lack or loss of identity? Do you find yourself constantly comparing yourself to others? If so, ask God to show you how much He loves you and wants you to find your true identity in Him.

You may want to take a look at an "in Christ" declaration (at the end of the book) that I've developed over the years. Why not take a moment to declare these truths over yourself? You could copy this list and make it your own, putting it somewhere prominent, such as your fridge or bathroom mirror.

DAY 3

Security and belonging

"I will say of the Lord, 'He is my refuge and my fortress, my God, in whom I trust.'"

PSALM 91:1

We're continuing our theme of developing the right mindset to live well. Yesterday we began by looking at the foundational importance of knowing who we really are—that is, getting an accurate perception of our true identity. Today, I want to focus on something that relates to this, which is our need for real security and belonging. As human beings, we have a natural desire for safety and security, yet we live in a world that is full of challenge and uncertainty. We may feel temporarily secure until crises come—whether they be global (like the coronavirus pandemic), or personal (such as an unexpected health, financial, or relational challenge). Suddenly we become aware that the things we previously put our security in can no longer hold us up. So where do we turn for our true security?

On one level, the answer lies in our relationships with other people. It's a well-known fact that people who have a sense of security and belonging in a family or friendship group are more likely to weather the storms of life. But given that human relationships are subject to change, is there somewhere else we can turn for a perfect and permanent sense of security and belonging?

A century ago, an ocean liner sank off the southwest coast of England, taking many people down with it. A 16-year-old galley boy, who was tossed up along the rugged shore, survived by clinging to a rock all night long. When he was finally rescued, he was asked, "Didn't you shake as you were clinging all night to that rock?" The boy replied, "Yes, of course. But the rock never shook once."[5] The great news is that even in a changing world and in tough and insecure situations, there is an unshakeable rock that we can cling to: Almighty God. As the psalmist put it: "The LORD is my rock, my fortress and my deliverer; my God is my rock, in whom I take refuge" (Psalm 18:2). We can have a similar sense of security if we will make the Lord God our rock and our refuge.

Elijah is a great illustration of this. He lived in a very challenging time. Israel as a nation was in sharp spiritual decline, with Baal worship becoming increasingly popular. Elijah was called to bring a message to a stubborn king and queen and a wayward people, to reject Baal and turn back to the true and living God. As such, he spent much of his time being hidden from the threat of royal retribution. Added to that, because of a drought (that he had prophesied), he faced continual challenges to his sense of material security. Yet if we read the narrative of these early years of his ministry, we'll see time and again Elijah demonstrating a secure and confident trust in God to protect and provide for him—even in the midst of the most challenging of circumstances.

This makes for a fascinating contrast with his outlook in 1 Kings 19, where he had temporarily taken his eyes off the Lord, literally running in fear for his life with all sense of security lost. The lessons are obvious. True security comes from putting our trust in God, whereas insecurity comes from trusting in our surroundings. In the words of Dr. Neil Anderson: "The key to understanding security is learning to relate to the eternal, not the temporal. Insecurity is caused by depending upon temporal things we have no right or ability to control."[6] These temporal things could be physical places, financial gain, or earthly relationships, all of which are shaky foundations on which to build our security.

This reference to being secure and yet not in control of everything is very significant. At the beginning of the coronavirus pandemic, I heard Christian psychologist Dr. Henry Cloud talk about how in such crisis situations, we as human beings naturally struggle with feelings of insecurity, partly related to a loss of control. His suggestion was to make two lists: one concerning things that we can't control, the other things that we can control.[7] So that's what I did. On my first list, I wrote things I can't control like the spread of the virus (beyond reasonable social distancing), when lockdown will ease, when a vaccine will be found, or how the global economy will be affected. On my other list, I wrote things like, "I am responsible for my thought life, my relationships, and my work." Compiling this list and revisiting it has been a key for me enjoying a balanced posture of peaceful proactivity, underpinned by a sense that ultimately God was and is in charge of my life—now and eternally.

This simple exercise highlights how we can take practical steps to develop the right mindset for living well. Some of these steps directly relate to the tips we mentioned on Day 1 (practice meditation and mindfulness; take control of your thoughts; develop the habit of casting your cares on the Lord). I find that as a Christian, spending time every day with God in quiet reflection, reading the Bible, praying, journaling, and being still, helps me enormously. Every time I come into His presence, I can offload worries and concerns onto Him, and receive a reminder that He is a perfect Father, the eternal, unchanging God, who is my only sure and safe refuge. One of my favorite parts of the Bible that brings this home is Psalm 91:1–2, where the psalmist says: "Whoever dwells in the shelter of the Most High will rest in the shadow of the Almighty. I will say of the LORD, 'He is my refuge and my fortress, my God, in whom I trust.'" Here's the promise for those who make the Lord their refuge: "His huge outstretched arms protect you—under them you're perfectly safe; his arms fend off all harm" (Psalm 91:3–4 *The Message).*

REFLECT & RESPOND

Spend some time with God and offer to Him any insecurity you may be feeling. If helpful, write out the two lists related to control and responsibility. You may then want to read Psalm 91 out loud over yourself and over others who you know need His security and protection. As you do, expect the Lord to minister a sense of peace and security deep within you. Write down any specific verses that particularly speak to you and carry them with you throughout the day.

DAY 4

"The Lord is my shepherd, I lack nothing. He makes me lie down in green pastures, he leads me beside quiet waters, he refreshes my soul."

PSALM 23:1–2

Depleted or replenished?

Having laid a foundation of knowing our true identity and knowing where we can find security and belonging, over the next few days we'll look at the second key perspective of knowing where we're really at, which relates to our self-awareness. Growing in self-awareness has been key to my increased wellness over the past few years, and I believe it is critical for all of us.

Even if we have an increasing sense of our identity in Christ, we're still human beings and we all face a natural tendency to get depleted. If we are unaware of where we're really at and don't take active steps to get replenished, the consequences can be serious—stress, depression, or even complete burnout.

Elijah is a case in point. The picture painted by the writer of 1 Kings, just prior to Elijah's collapse, is of a man of great strength. Whether it be his huge victory against the false prophets on Mount Carmel, his successful prayer for the drought to end, or his outrunning the king's chariot under the power of the Spirit, everything looks well! There is nothing to forewarn us that he's about to suddenly burn out in such a dramatic way. While the text doesn't reveal to us his state of mind at this point, it may be that the toll of the previous years and the aftermath of the encounter with the prophets of Baal had left him depleted and vulnerable to the sudden attack from Queen Jezebel. The extent of his collapse in the desert indicates that Elijah had likely been in a state of what author Ruth Haley Barton calls being "dangerously tired."[8]

This doesn't necessarily mean that if we're feeling tired, we're in danger of burnout. I often feel a kind of "good tired" after a busy day involved in productive work or an extensive time of exercise. But there is a tiredness, a chronic fatigue, which may build over a number of weeks, months, or even years—and it isn't always immediately obvious. I know from both personal experience and leading others that a key to avoiding burnout is to develop self-awareness and to be alert to when we begin to feel "dangerously tired." I've never hit a low like Elijah, but there have been seasons when I've felt particularly depleted. The first was in the four years after Karen and I had moved to the city of Peterborough to start what is now KingsGate Community Church. In those initial years, the pressures bore down on us in all areas, resulting in us feeling exhausted much of the time. The second was 15–20 years later, when we were involved in an intense battle to buy land in order to build our church facility. Added to that was the blessing but pressure of fast growth once we finally moved into our new building. We both came into that new season feeling very weary indeed. The third time was in 2016, when Karen and I realized that we were experiencing long-term tiredness. It wasn't that anything in particular had gone wrong; we were simply beginning to feel depleted from three decades of ministry and needed a new season of replenishment.

Through each of these seasons, I've had to grow in an understanding of my human limitations and awareness of how I'm really doing. With the Lord's help, I've been able to take preventative measures in order to avoid more serious exhaustion, depression, or burnout. Throughout this book, I'll be sharing some of the lessons I've learned and some of the rhythms of replenishment that I've embraced.

You may, like me, receive huge benefits from taking such preventative action. You might, however, be in a more desperate state, feeling completely exhausted, depressed, or near burnout and needing more remedial help—in which case, Elijah's example and story could be particularly pertinent.

REFLECT & RESPOND

Whether you're doing great or feeling very depleted, take a few moments to pray, thanking God that He understands your humanity. As you go throughout your day, take moments to consider where you're really at. Invite God to refresh you and teach you rhythms of replenishment.

DAY 5

A faith (not fear) mindset

"For God has not given us a spirit of fear, but of power and of love and of a sound mind."

2 Timothy 1:7 (NKJV)

Today we are continuing with our theme of developing the right mindset to live well and the importance of growing in self-awareness, by asking whether we're viewing our lives and circumstances through the lens of faith or fear.

Faith is closely linked with trust. It involves putting your whole weight on something. As I am writing this, I am sitting in a chair and I have faith that it will hold me up! Rather than putting our weight or trust in things that are uncertain in life, we need to put our faith in God our rock, who alone is totally trustworthy and reliable. When we do this, we can experience peace and mental wellness, even in tough times.

The opposite is also true. There's something about fear that has the power to completely destabilize us. While some fear can be a positive means of protecting us from physical and emotional danger, fear also has the potential to become irrational and destructive. Sudden bad news—a health scare, a financial situation, a relational fallout, a family member in trouble, a challenging work situation—can cause us to lose our equilibrium. Unsurprisingly, when the coronavirus crisis suddenly hit the world in the first few months of 2020, the first response of so many was fear, with widespread panic-buying as a common reaction.

Whether we walk in faith or fear has a tremendous impact on our mental health and overall wellbeing. Take Elijah, for example. He went from displaying tremendous faith to experiencing paralyzing fear. If we look back through the narrative of 1 Kings 17–18, we see a great picture of true faith in action.

Time and again we hear this phrase: "the word of the LORD came to Elijah" (see 1 Kings 17:2, 8; 18:1). As a result, Elijah boldly spoke out and acted on what the Lord said to him, resulting in amazing miracles and great spiritual victories. However, just as bold faith was a key to his success, so great fear was a major factor in his sudden fall. The author of this fear was Elijah's archenemy, Jezebel, the wife of King Ahab, who used words of fear and intimidation to devastating effect. We read: "So Jezebel sent a messenger to Elijah to say, 'May the gods deal with me, be it ever so severely, if by this time tomorrow I do not make your life like that of one of them'" (1 Kings 19:2). Elijah had had the prophets of Baal killed, so this was a blatant threat of revenge from Jezebel. At this news, Elijah, vulnerable and exhausted, panicked: "Elijah was afraid and ran for his life" (1 Kings 19:3).

From Elijah's example and the rest of Scripture, it's clear that the key to whether we're walking in faith or fear concerns who or what we're listening to. I believe we need to make a daily choice to do two things:

Feed our faith. Romans 10:17 tells us that "faith comes by hearing, and hearing by the word of God" (NKJV). Unsurprisingly, Elijah's faith was fueled by hearing from God. If we want to similarly live by faith, we need to spend regular time in God's Word and learn to cultivate an intimate walk with the Spirit (see Days 26–27 for more on listening to God). As we hear God speak, faith comes to us.

Starve our fears. In 2 Timothy 1:7 (NKJV) we read that "God has not given us a spirit of fear, but of power and of love and of a sound mind." We really can exercise self-control over what we allow to come into our minds, starving our fears by silencing the Jezebel-like voices that can rob us of peace and wellbeing. We also need to recognize that behind human voices or our own negative thoughts, we have a spiritual enemy, the devil, who uses the fear of both real and imagined situations to derail us. The good news is that if we turn to God, who is far greater, and re-surrender our thoughts and lives to Him, we don't have to succumb to this fear. As we read in the New Testament letter of James, we have these clear exhortations: "Submit yourselves, then, to God. Resist the devil, and he will flee from you. Come near to God and he will come near to you" (James 4:7–8).

This whole subject of fear, and our need to be free from it, is such a big issue that we will be revisiting it and looking at how it impacts our emotional wellbeing (see Day 16).

REFLECT & RESPOND

Take a few moments to write down your primary fears. Invite the Holy Spirit to help you identify the reasons for your greatest fear. Then, command the fear to go, in Jesus' name! As you go about your day, thank God for His promise in 2 Timothy 1:7.

DAY 6

An overcoming (not overwhelmed) mindset

"But they who wait for the Lord shall renew their strength; they shall mount up with wings like eagles; they shall run and not be weary; they shall walk and not faint."

ISAIAH 40:31 (ESV)

During a talk he gave at the Global Leadership Summit in 2013,[9] Henry Cloud explained how, during the financial meltdown of 2007 and 2008, he was working with hedge fund managers who were completely traumatized by the sudden collapse in the financial markets.

Many had lost everything and were being blamed for the whole crash, too. Buffeted by these external circumstances and feeling powerless to bring change, the brains of these financiers began to view the world in three predictable ways: what Cloud calls "the three Ps" (based on the work of Martin Seligman). The first P is "Personal," where we interpret a crisis in a personal way: *I think I'm a failure; it's all my fault.* The second P is "Pervasive," where we go further: *Everything I do is a failure.* The third P is "Permanent," when we end up thinking, *It will always be like this*, and we feel completely overwhelmed. So how can we reverse the spiral? Cloud recommends three things:

1. **Dispute the negative thinking.** Since most of these personal, permanent, and pervasive thoughts will be false, naming them, writing them down, and disputing them with the truth (especially from the Bible) will largely cause them to dissipate.

2. **Get back control.** This can be done, for example, as I referred to in Day 3, by writing down lists of things you cannot and can control and by choosing not to take responsibility for the former but acting on the latter.

3. **Connect with others.** When in a crisis, having meaningful relationships is key, as we shall see when we cover relationships later in this book.

The good news is that when it comes to feeling overwhelmed, God is still present to help us. Once again, Elijah's story is instructive. Here was someone who, in his early ministry years, displayed a remarkable ability to overcome tough situations. Yet in the face of Jezebel's threat, he ran in fear for his life, ended up in the desert, came to a bush, sat down under it, and prayed that he might die: "'I have had enough, LORD,' he said. 'Take my life; I am no better than my ancestors.' Then he lay down under the bush and fell asleep" (1 Kings 19:4–5). If ever there was a picture of someone feeling overwhelmed, this is it. It highlights the importance of James's reminder that this overcomer, this great man of faith and prayer, was also "a human being, even as we are" (James 5:17). So be encouraged: feeling overwhelmed doesn't make you odd, it simply confirms that you're human!

Thankfully, this isn't the end of the story for Elijah or for us. Because God had a plan for his and our replenishment, the overwhelmed can be overcomers again.

So, what can we learn from Elijah about how to develop an overcoming rather than an overwhelmed mindset? There are two things to highlight here:

Don't panic. The contrast between Elijah's calmness under pressure during his early ministry years and his fear-based panic in 1 Kings 19 is striking. It emphasizes how, especially when we're feeling physically, emotionally, and spiritually tired, we're much more likely to react poorly to seemingly adverse circumstances or sudden bad news (such as a health report, relational crisis, or financial downturn). This immediate, short-term, fear-based response causes us to take our eyes off the Lord, leading to feelings of being overwhelmed. By contrast we need to learn to ...

Be patient. The God-confidence that Elijah exuded in his early ministry years meant that he not only had the faith to speak out what God was saying to him, but he also had the patience to wait for the promise to come to pass. This issue of patience can be challenging for us today, especially in our culture where we have become conditioned to expect things to happen quickly—even instantly. That means many of us have a real problem in waiting for almost anything! This can rob us of the ability to step back in a crisis and develop a long-term perspective. By contrast, patience is a vital "twin" which, along with faith, enables us to stand firm in any situation and ultimately to inherit all that God has promised to us (see Hebrews 6:12).

As we grow in our identity and security in Christ and develop a faith-not-fear mindset, we will be less easily overwhelmed and will increase our resilience and readiness to embrace life's opportunities and overcome each of its challenges.

REFLECT & RESPOND

Cast your mind back to a recent time when you felt overwhelmed. How did you feel physically or emotionally? What were your actions and what was the outcome? If you're still struggling, take comfort and courage from Elijah, the overcomer, the one who had the God-confidence to rise up in adversity and wait in patient faith for God's word to come to pass. Take time to come before God and invite Him to strengthen and restore your confidence in Him.

DAY 7

A growth (not fixed) mindset

"I can do all things through Him who strengthens me."

PHILIPPIANS 4:13 (NASB)

Today we come to the third perspective for developing a mindset to live well, which concerns the importance of knowing that no matter where we're at, we can change!

Christian evangelist Nick Vujicic was born with tetra-amelia syndrome, a rare disorder characterized by the absence of all four limbs. After struggling mentally and physically, he found a way to deal with his condition, resulting in him establishing his own non-profit organization, Life Without Limbs, and becoming a world-renowned motivational speaker. Rather than sharing his complaints as you might expect, he talks about how he has developed an optimistic outlook on life. This remarkable man who has no limbs teaches people with all four limbs (and therefore so many more opportunities) how to enjoy life, how not to give up, and how to be happy. Here are a few of his sayings:

"The greatest disability is not having no arms and legs; the greatest disability is your *mind*."

"Are you going to make the choice to get up, rather than give up?"

"Don't be afraid of failure. Every time you fall down, every time you fail, you learn something new ... you've learned how not to do something. Well then, learn from it and move on!"[10]

Nick is a wonderful example of someone who has developed what researcher Dr. Carol Dweck calls a growth mindset. Her studies revealed that there are two opposing mindsets. With a fixed mindset, people believe their qualities are fixed traits and therefore cannot change. Alternatively, with a growth mindset, people have an underlying belief that their learning and intelligence can grow with time and experience. When people believe they can get smarter, they realize that their effort has an effect on their success, so they put in extra time, leading to higher achievement.[11] Another author summarizes it this way: "The growth mindset allows us to unleash the potential we have by applying our effort and energy to develop our abilities and talents. ... The high achievers in society, and in our schools, are those who stretch their abilities further than others. It's not necessarily the case that they have more ability, they just stretch them a little further."[12] Albert Einstein is alleged to have put it the most succinctly: "The measure of intelligence is the ability to change."

So, before we look at each of the six areas of our lives in more detail, I encourage you to approach each one with a mindset of proactivity and growth, even if you feel like you're currently stuck. In fact, because the areas are interrelated, it's important not to neglect any of them.

You may not be particularly physically fit, but attending to this area will not only dramatically increase your physical energy, it will potentially have a huge impact on other key areas such as your emotional and spiritual wellbeing. You may not feel emotionally healthy right now, but addressing root issues will considerably increase your sense of emotional peace and will have a big bearing on your physical, spiritual, relational, and vocational wellbeing. You may not feel spiritually strong yet, but focusing here will lead to increased satisfaction and wellbeing in the very deepest part of you, as well as bringing an increased sense of identity, security, and hope that will affect every other area of your life. You may not feel that you are currently enjoying sufficient relational connection or harmony, but investing in other people will dramatically improve not only your relationships but your emotional wellbeing, too. You may not yet have found your vocational "sweet spot," but gaining new clarity in this area will also benefit you spiritually, emotionally, and probably financially, too.

While acknowledging the importance of a growth mindset and of being proactive in all areas of our lives, the great news is that we're not alone on our journey to live well! Rather, we have an all-loving, all-powerful God who knows us better than we know ourselves and who wants to help us change. This applies whether we are doing well or whether, like Elijah, we're living in the red zone and need more serious help. In his case, he had completely lost any sense of get up and go and, having dismissed his only companion, his servant, he was completely isolated. Thankfully, God had not forgotten him, lovingly sending an angel to tell him (twice) to get up, and we read: "So he [Elijah] got up" (1 Kings 19:5–8). This is so encouraging. While we may not necessarily experience an angel coming to us, we can have something even better, which is the presence of God Himself, indwelling us 24/7 for the rest of our lives. When we feel down and out, He is there strengthening and helping us to get up every time we fall, spurring us on to ongoing change and growth.

This reminds me of a time when I was at primary school, running in my first 800-meter race. Halfway around, I found myself in the middle of the pack with lots of runners ahead. I suddenly decided I could run faster, so I started accelerating and overtaking runner after runner. As I did so, I became aware of a voice from the sidelines shouting out, "Come on, boy, you can do it!" It was the voice of my dad. At the sound of his encouragement, it was as if my legs were suddenly supercharged and I started overtaking the other lead runners, before finally collapsing over the line at the shoulder of the best runner in the school—a very close second, having run the greatest race of my life—spurred on by my dad's encouragement.

The wonderful news is that there is someone far greater than my dad, who is available to each and every one of us: our Father in heaven. Through Jesus, and His Holy Spirit living within us, He is cheering us on to greater growth and wellness in every area of our lives.

REFLECT & RESPOND

Given the interrelatedness of all these different areas, take a few moments to revisit your life dashboard. Then pray and ask for God's help to move forward in all areas, especially those where you feel you are stuck or struggling most. Remember, with God's help and your determination, you can and will change!

LIVE WELL PHYSICALLY

DAY 8

Your body matters

"You are not your own; you were bought at a price. Therefore honor God with your bodies."

1 CORINTHIANS 6:19–20

In 1943, the psychologist Abraham Maslow produced what became a highly influential paper around the subject of the hierarchy of human needs.[1] He imagined a pyramid representing our five basic needs, each of which is dependent on the other. At the base of the pyramid, and foundational to the rest, are our physiological needs such as the need for food, water, air, and rest. Only when these needs are satisfied can we move confidently on to the other needs of safety, belonging, esteem, and what Maslow labeled self-actualization. While his findings have been the cause of much debate, there is a broad agreement today that our first or most basic needs are physiological.

Many studies bear this out. Having worked for 25 years to help great athletes perform at the highest level, Jim Loehr and Tony Schwartz wrote a book in which they sought to apply these learnings to high-performing people and organizations. Published under the title *The Power of Full Engagement*, the premise of the book is contained in the subtitle: "Managing Energy, Not Time, Is the Key to High Performance and Personal Renewal." They rightly emphasize the interrelatedness of different areas of our lives and start by looking at the physical: "The importance of physical energy seems obvious for athletes, construction workers, and farmers. ... In reality, physical energy is the fundamental source of fuel, even if our work is almost completely sedentary. It not only lies at the heart of alertness and vitality but also affects our ability to manage our emotions, sustain our concentration, think creatively, and even maintain our commitment to whatever mission we are on."[2]

This emphasis on the importance of our bodies, and of the foundational importance of physical energy, totally coincides with the worldview of the Bible.

God is Spirit, yet He chose to create a physical universe and gave us physical bodies in which to live. It is also of supreme significance that Jesus Christ, the Son of God, became a real human being with a physical body. He was physically crucified, was physically resurrected, and is now at the right hand of God in heaven, ruling and reigning in a glorified, resurrected physical body. As if that's not enough, the Bible tells us that when Christ returns, He's coming to bring a new or renewed heavens and earth and that those who love Him will live on this new earth in glorified, resurrected, bodies, too—forever!

After that theological interjection(!), let me make this very down to earth by simply saying: your body matters. It matters to God and it matters to you and, as Loehr and Schwartz rightly emphasize, renewing our physical health and energy affects every other area of our lives. Many models of counseling start in the physical before working their way into the other "dials"—and sometimes the reason we feel, for example, emotionally empty, is because we need help physically.

That's why, as we shall see in the next few days, when God saw His burnt-out prophet Elijah, He first ministered to his physical needs.

REFLECT & RESPOND

Pause and take time to thank God for the gift of your physical body. If appropriate, ask Him to forgive you where you have neglected the care and renewal of your physical strength. Ask for Him to help and empower you as you journey toward living well physically.

DAY 9

"Come to me, all you who are weary and burdened, and I will give you rest."

MATTHEW 11:28

Physical replenishment

The Reverend George Whitefield is one of my personal heroes. He was an amazing eighteenth-century evangelist, who was the human catalyst for one of the greatest Christian revivals in history known as the Great Awakening, when hundreds of thousands came to Christ in Britain and America. One of the places he preached was Charleston, South Carolina. This is an excerpt from his journal written in the summer of 1740:

> *"People seemed to come from all parts, and the Word came with convincing power ... I hastened to Charleston; but my body was so exceeding weak, and the sun shone so intensely hot that I lay for a considerable time, almost breathless and dead. ... But God comforted me; and, being thereby strengthened in*

> *the inner man, I preached … with more freedom and power than could have been expected, considering the great weakness of my body."*[3]

Here was a man in a revival situation, ministering the Word of God with great spiritual power, while at the same time neglecting his physical wellness. He came from a school of thought that you should burn yourself out for God—and he literally did. He hit the peak of his influence in his mid-to-late twenties before increasing ill-health in his thirties and forties limited his effectiveness. He died prematurely at 56. A truly great man, but one who neglected his physical health.

This example highlights that it's not enough for us just to focus on spiritual and vocational matters. Since wellbeing is holistic, we also need to attend to issues like our physical health. As has often been said, we need to take care of our bodies, because they are the only place we have to live!

This physical aspect was the starting point for God's plan for Elijah. As we read the account in 1 Kings 19, it's clear that Elijah was physically exhausted. We are not told exactly why. It may have been partly due to the huge mental, emotional, and spiritual pressure that he had been under through his confrontation with the prophets of Baal and the insidious threat from Queen Jezebel. It may also have been a result of him just physically overdoing it. From the intensity of the Mount Carmel encounter, Elijah initially journeyed from Carmel to Jezreel (17–30 miles) aided by the supernatural strength of God. However, he then fled in a state of panic from Jezreel all the way down to the south, to Beersheba in Judah. This was a journey of 100 miles, which probably included a mixture of running, walking, and stumbling. Then, from the small settlement in Beersheba, he went on a further day's journey into the wilderness and immediately fell asleep. In light of all this, it seems obvious that a key factor in Elijah's burnout was physical exhaustion—so God started with his physical replenishment. As Ruth Haley Barton put it: "God did not waste time trying to deal with him intellectually or even spiritually, because it wouldn't have done any good. He began by dealing with Elijah's physical weariness and depletion—he let Elijah sleep. Then he woke Elijah up when it was time to eat and drink, provided food and water for him, told him to go back to sleep, and then started the process all over again."[4]

It's the same with us: God's plan for our thriving often starts with attending to our physical replenishment.

REFLECT & RESPOND

Consider whether your physical dial is in the green, yellow, or red zone. What do you need to do to help improve the place where you live (your body)? Invite the Lord to help you take the right next steps toward greater physical wellness.

DAY 10

"In peace I will lie down and sleep, for you alone, Lord, make me dwell in safety."

PSALMS 4:8

Sleep matters

Over the next three days, we will be focusing on the three most important elements of our physical wellness: good sleep, healthy eating, and regular exercise.

According to the Mental Health Foundation: "Sleep is as important to our health as eating, drinking, and breathing. It allows our bodies to repair themselves and our brains to consolidate our memories and process information. Poor sleep is linked to physical problems such as a weakened immune system and mental health problems such as anxiety and depression."[5] The benefits of a good night's sleep include improved attention and learning, and increased emotional, mental, and relational wellbeing.

Clearly, sleep matters—a lot! That's why, as we saw yesterday, the first thing that the exhausted Elijah did was sleep: "he lay down under the bush and fell asleep" (1 Kings 19:5). Although in this instance an angel appeared to him and woke him to give something that was also essential, food (see Day 11), he then allowed him to lie down and fall asleep again. Throughout the Bible, we see that God the Creator is fully aware of our need for good sleep. Here's one example from the Psalms: "In peace I will lie down and sleep, for you alone, LORD, make me dwell in safety" (Psalm 4:8).

Over the last few years, the importance of sleep has been brought home to me. Whether it was due to a change of season (I'm getting older!) or internal pressures from overload, there was a particular time when I found myself struggling to get sufficient sleep. I would either have a problem getting to sleep, frequently wake and be unable to get back to sleep, or regularly wake much too early. While I didn't stop sleeping altogether—and thankfully it didn't get to the point of being so bad as to cause me any significant physical or emotional problems—I was aware, far too often, of going into the day functioning on less than a full tank. Recognizing the importance of sleeping well—without getting anxious about it—I have made some important practical changes, some of which are included in the list below. Since worrying about not sleeping only makes things worse, if I'm unable to sleep, I often get up and do something non-screen related such as reading or journaling, and then go back to bed when feeling sleepy. It may just be my goal-oriented personality, but I've found a sleep tracker helpful. This not only records whether I'm getting enough sleep but also measures the quality of that sleep, broken down into REM sleep, light sleep, and deep sleep. It even measures how restful my sleep is based on my heart rate.

You may be in a similar situation of needing better sleep. If so, here's a comprehensive list of "Twelve Tips for Healthy Sleep" from best-selling author Matthew Walker:[6]

1. Stick to a sleep schedule.
2. Exercise, but not too late in the day.
3. Avoid caffeine and nicotine. (Caffeine can take eight hours to wear off fully.)
4. Avoid alcoholic drinks before bed.
5. Avoid large meals and beverages late at night.
6. If possible, avoid medicines that delay or disrupt your sleep.
7. Don't take naps after 3 p.m.
8. Relax before bed.
9. Take a hot bath before bed.
10. Aim for a dark, cool, gadget-free bedroom.

11. Have the right sunlight exposure.
12. Don't lie in bed awake.

In addition to some of these practical changes, the greatest impact on my sleep has been the sense of wellness that I've begun to experience mentally and emotionally. Even though I would still like to sleep longer, I am now enjoying a greater quantity and quality of sleep than I have in years!

There is clearly a link between our trust in God, our inner peace, and being able to truly rest. As the psalmist put it: "I have calmed and quieted my soul, like a weaned child with its mother" (Psalm 131:2 ESV). This beautiful picture of a satiated child resting against its mother is a wonderful illustration of how we can learn to rest in the loving protection of Almighty God and adopt a posture that will bring peace to our souls and help us enter into better and more restful sleep. As has often been said, there is no pillow as soft as a clear conscience!

REFLECT & RESPOND

I encourage you to take some time to ponder these verses: Psalms 4:8; 127:2; and 131:2. If you are sleeping well, thank God for this gift. If you are struggling with getting enough quality sleep, ask the Lord to help you, and be open to making physical or emotional adjustments to enable you to sleep better. If you wake up and can't get back to sleep, try praying!

DAY 11

"He gives food to every creature."

PSALM 136:25

Eating well

Many years ago, I unknowingly filled up my wife's diesel car with gasoline. It wasn't until I tried to leave the station that I realized there was a problem. The ensuing cost and disruption of getting a mechanic out to drain the tank (and the lively conversation when I got home) taught me a valuable lesson!

Food and drink are like fuel to our bodies. If we put the wrong type of fuel into our system, it will have adverse effects. Conversely, getting enough of the right proteins, carbohydrates, fats, vitamins, minerals, and water is essential for our physical health, which is the foundation for wellbeing in every other area of our lives. Drinking enough water and eating healthily have obvious benefits, such as greater energy levels, better sleep, and enhanced emotional peace.

So, it's unsurprising that after allowing Elijah to sleep, the very next thing that God did for his depleted servant was give him a good meal. The tenderness in this incident is striking. Elijah had just laid down, exhausted and suicidal, and was asleep: "All at once an angel touched him and said, 'Get up and eat.' He looked around, and there by his head was some bread baked over hot coals, and a jar of water. He ate and drank and then lay down again" (1 Kings 19:5–6). Wow! Here is Elijah in the desert, ready to die, and yet an angel comes to him, touches him, and provides a meal of freshly baked bread and water. Still tired, Elijah "ate and drank and then lay down again. The angel of the LORD came back a second time and touched him and said, 'Get up and eat, for the journey is too much for you.' So he got up and ate and drank. ***Strengthened by that food***, he traveled for forty days and forty nights until he reached Horeb, the mountain of God" (1 Kings 19:6–8, my italics).

God had a plan for Elijah's refreshment which went way beyond the physical—and which included an all-important encounter at the mountain of God. However, in order for Elijah to be ready to make that journey, he had to first be strengthened physically. The fact that he was able to journey for 40 days through a land that was mostly desert, on the strength of that double angel-feast, suggests that this meal was something special!

We may never in this life get to the point of needing our food to be provided by angels. However, we do know from the rest of Scripture that since God designed us to be physical beings, He knows our need for physical food and drink. Right from the beginning, we see a picture of God placing Adam and Eve in the garden, which they were to tend and from which they could eat. This same care for our basic needs is highlighted in the Lord's Prayer, where Jesus instructs us to pray to our Father, "Give us today our daily bread" (Matthew 6:11). We'll explore more of how God provides for us when we look at how to live well financially, but for now, know that God is interested in us having the right sustenance for our physical wellbeing. That's His part. Our part is to take responsibility to ensure that we are putting the right physical fuel into our bodies. So, what does this look like in practice? Here are a few suggestions:

- Make sure that you're drinking enough water. Water is essential for our rehydration and wellness.
- Make sure (unless you're fasting) that you don't skip breakfast. It's generally recognized that we need the right amount of "fuel" at the start of the day.

- Avoid eating big meals late at night. This is partly because we have less time to digest and burn off the calories which can affect our weight and our sleep.
- Make sure you have a balanced diet that includes an abundant daily intake of fruit and vegetables.
- Try not to eat too much! Even if you have a balanced diet, it's possible to become unhealthy because your portion sizes are too large.

As has often been said, when it comes to our bodies, we are what we eat!

REFLECT & RESPOND

Start by thanking God that He cares for you and wants to provide for you. Then ask for His help and guidance as you review your eating and drinking habits. Look over the list above and identify one key change that you can adopt right away. (If you have an eating disorder, please seek professional medical help.)

DAY 12

"Offer your bodies as a living sacrifice, holy and pleasing to God."

ROMANS 12:1

Exercise

The benefits of physical exercise, along with the need to stretch regularly, are obvious and well-known. For us in modern Western cultures, without falling into the trap of making an idol of exercise and our physique, we need to be very intentional about exercise—the gain is worth the pain! Exercise has been proven to increase our energy, enhance our mental health, and help prevent many diseases. As John F. Kennedy put it: "Physical fitness is not only one of the most important keys to a healthy body, it is the basis of dynamic and creative intellectual activity." Elsewhere, John J. Ratey writes about "how exercise cues the building blocks of learning in the brain; how it affects mood, anxiety, and attention; how it guards against stress and reverses some of the effects of aging in the brain."[7]

Given these considerable physiological, intellectual, and emotional benefits, it's important that we approach this subject of physical exercise with a growth mindset. If you've tried and failed in this area before, don't be discouraged. Know that you can change and make progress!

If you need added motivation, here are three of the reasons why I exercise. First, it helps me feel good. If I am a bit jaded physically, low emotionally, struggling spiritually, or just in need of fresh ideas and creativity, I instinctively take a quick walk. With my body freshly re-energized, I invariably come back feeling refreshed and revitalized.

Second, I experience increased levels of physical energy and strength. I find that regular, daily, and varied exercise has a compounding effect. While I don't feel fitter or stronger from just one or two sessions, in a relatively short space of time I'm aware that I have greater energy, capacity, and ability to focus.

Third, I know that I am investing in my long-term health and physical wellbeing. I take seriously the fact that life is a gift from God, and I want to make the most of this one life that I have. I also hate being sick and want to live as long as it is God's will for me to do so. This helps motivate me to exercise, even when I don't feel like it.

It's important that we attend to this matter of exercise, especially if, like me, your job is not primarily physical. It's also worth bearing in mind that we live in a culture where, unlike Elijah, most of our modes of transportation require little or no physical activity.

It's interesting that in 1 Kings 19, God didn't immediately meet with Elijah in the desert. The main reason is that He wanted to bring him to the mountain where He had previously revealed Himself to Moses. In other words, it was for the purpose of a spiritual encounter. However, without reading too much into the story, I wonder whether there were other supplementary physical and emotional benefits of this journey, too.

What is clear for us today is that, without us needing to go on 40-day hikes(!), regular physical exercise done in the right way is highly beneficial not just to our bodies but our whole sense of wellbeing. So, what guidelines can we adopt when it comes to getting physical exercise? Here are a few:

- **Invest the time.** The general advice is that we need to be physically active, getting at least 30 minutes of moderate aerobic exercise five times a week, as well as some kind of muscle strengthening, such as push-ups, weights, or gardening.
- **Make it fun.** If you love going to the gym, go for it! But you can get equally beneficial exercise from regular walks, bike rides, mountain climbs, and sports. It's largely true that if you don't enjoy it, you're less likely to stick with it.

- **Don't compare.** We are all different and at different stages of physical fitness and age. Don't let yourself be discouraged by some kind of ideal of how you should look and what you should do. Instead ...
- **Take small steps.** If maintaining a brisk walk for 30 minutes is a struggle for you, don't start by trying to run a marathon! Instead, start where you're at, add exercise incrementally, and keep at it.

REFLECT & RESPOND

You might like to re-look at my motivations for exercise and consider your own. If you are hardly exercising at all, think about one thing you might enjoy that could get you started. Would you benefit more from doing exercise alone or with others? If alone, could you make the time more interesting by watching or listening to a podcast or an energizing playlist? Think about what time or times would work best for you. Try to set a realistic goal, share it with others, and then get started. Don't be discouraged if you fail. Keep going—it will be worth it!

DAY 13

Physical healing

"Beloved, I pray that you may prosper in all things and be in health, just as your soul prospers."

3 JOHN 2 (NKJV)

In thinking about how to live well physically, we've focused so far on what we can practically do to see an increase in health and energy. However, I'm very conscious of the fact that right now you may be struggling not because of a lack of healthy disciplines, but because of either short-term or long-term sickness or disability. If that's the case, there is hope.

If we look back to God's overall plan for our wellbeing (or *shalom*), we see that sickness was never God's original intention. While this is not the time nor the place to fully unpack the challenging issue of suffering, it seems likely, in the light of Genesis 1–3, that much of what we suffer from today is broadly connected to the fact that we're currently living in a fallen world that is less than God's best.

God's consistent heart to heal people is revealed in the fact that not only is His name Yahweh-Shalom, "The LORD Is Peace [wellbeing]," but He is also Yahweh-Rapha, "The LORD Our Healer" (Exodus 15:26). In the Old Testament, there were two primary ways in which God brought health and healing to His people: first, as they obeyed the conditions of His covenant (see Exodus 15:26; 23:25), and second, as an act of His mercy through people who were anointed by the Spirit.

One of these anointed people was the prophet Elijah. The incident in question concerns the sickness and death of the widow's son. Elijah responded by taking the dead boy up to the room where he was staying and laying him on his bed: "Then he cried out to the LORD, 'LORD my God, have you brought tragedy even on this widow I am staying with, by causing her son to die?'" (Notice how personal and honest he is before God.) "Then he stretched himself out on the boy three times and cried out to the LORD, 'LORD my God, let this boy's life return to him!' The LORD heard Elijah's cry, and the boy's life returned to him, and he lived. Elijah picked up the child and carried him down from the room into the house. He gave him to his mother and said, 'Look, your son is alive!'" (1 Kings 17:20–23). What a wonderful picture of God's mercy and power at work!

Although this was a remarkable miracle, it wasn't the only Old Testament occasion of healing or resurrection. Many years later, for example, Elijah's successor, Elisha, performed a similar miracle, raising to life the son of a Shunammite woman (2 Kings 4:17–37).

Both these incidents point forward to the full manifestation of God's healing and miracle ministry in and through His Son, Jesus, centuries later. When Jesus resurrected the son of another widow in a town called Nain (likely very close to the place of Elisha's miracle), the people were "all filled with awe and praised God. 'A great prophet has appeared among us. ... God has come to help his people'" (Luke 7:16). Later, summarizing Jesus' remarkable ministry, the apostle Peter spoke of how "God anointed Jesus of Nazareth with the Holy Spirit and power, and ... he went around doing good and healing all who were under the power of the devil, because God was with him" (Acts 10:38).

The great news is that "Jesus Christ is the same yesterday and today and forever" (Hebrews 13:8). Having completed His earthly ministry, He died on the cross to pay the price for our sin and to undo all the effects of the Fall, before rising triumphantly over death. After the Holy Spirit was poured out on the day of Pentecost, the Church went out in His name and continued His healing and miracle ministry. Today, when we pray "Your Kingdom come, Your will be done," we are praying that the perfect reign of God might be established here and now—including healing—both for ourselves and for those around us, in Jesus' name. And even if we don't always experience healing in this life, we have the promise that when Jesus comes back, the reign of God will be fully and finally manifested and we will be physically resurrected as Jesus Himself was—not just as the boys in our miracle stories, who were raised and then eventually died (presumably as old men)—but with glorified, resurrected physical bodies that will live forever!

REFLECT & RESPOND

If you're weak or sick in any way, as well as taking practical steps to speed up natural healing processes, why not take time over these next few weeks to turn to God and ask Him to heal you, in Jesus' name? You can pray this great prayer over your life and the lives of people around you: "Beloved, I pray that you may prosper in all things and be in health, just as your soul prospers" (3 John 1:2 NKJV).

DAY 14

Habits for physical wellbeing

"So whether you eat or drink or whatever you do, do it all for the glory of God."

1 CORINTHIANS 10:31

As we conclude our week's look at how to live well physically, let's focus on our habits. The key to making continuous progress is to build repeatable habits. This applies in all areas of our lives, including the physical.

In *The Power of Habit*, Charles Duhigg defines habits as "the choices all of us deliberately make at some point, and then stop thinking about but continue doing, often every day." Studies have shown that it is "actually people's unthinking routines—or habits—that form the bedrock of everyday life," with around 45% of our everyday actions performed almost daily and in the same location.[8] This applies to both good and bad habits. So, if we can build good habits in terms of routines and rhythms for sleep, diet, and exercise, it could have an exponential impact on our long-term physical health.

What is also clear is that we don't have to make huge leaps in order to enjoy major change. Instead, it is the small but powerful incremental changes that can have a massive and compounding effect on our lives—something best-selling author James Clear calls "atomic habits," which are small steps that incrementally make a huge difference. Clear writes: "Whether it is losing weight, building a business, writing a book, winning a championship, or achieving any other goal, we put pressure on ourselves to make some earth-shattering improvement. ... Meanwhile, improving by 1 percent isn't particularly notable ... but it can be far more meaningful, especially in the long run. The difference a tiny improvement can make over time is outstanding."[9]

Based on this principle of incremental change through small improvement, Clear lays out three steps of habit change:

- Reminder (the trigger that initiates the behavior)
- Routine (the behavior itself; the action you take)
- Reward (the benefit you gain from doing the behavior)

So, how might we apply this to our need for better diet and regular exercise? Here are a few examples that come to mind:

- Reminder: Put out fruit in bowls where it's visible and accessible and put away sweets and treats; put out your sports shoes the night before or take your gym bag to work and keep it on the front seat of the car.
- Routine: Do some exercise before work and/or straight after work (start small if you're just beginning).
- Reward: Have an enjoyable and nourishing breakfast or come back and have a hot bath and read a favorite book, or listen to music or an edifying podcast.

The key is to get started, take small steps, and not give up when you temporarily fail.

As we bring our discussion of how to live well physically to a close and begin to look ahead, I want to share the story of one of our church members:

> *"Last autumn we studied Pastor Dave's series, God's Plan for Your Wellbeing. All of the topics were very relevant and helped me in many ways, but the greatest impact came from the message on physical*

wellbeing. I have been overweight—bordering obese—for at least five years, and despite gentle prodding from my wife, mother, family, and friends, I had resisted doing very much about it. God spoke to me that Sunday morning and armed with a spiritual prompt and some practical advice from the message, I started to take control of my diet and introduce some serious exercise. In just over two months, I had lost 13 lbs. in weight. I am still sticking to this new lifestyle, and at last count, I have lost 40 lbs. God gave me a determination and resilience in this matter that I never could have found in my own strength. I still have a little way to go, but I will get there. I have walked 2.356 million steps in the last six months at an average of nearly 13,000 steps per day and have cycled and used a home elliptical trainer regularly. I used two practical aids to help me: a step tracker and a calorie counter. Not only have I lost eight inches from my waist, but I've also lost fat from my face, neck, arms, legs, and even my fingers. I feel re-energized and less tired and have found that activity breeds activity. I thank God for speaking to me through the wellbeing series and for the difference it has made. As well as the physical improvements, my relational, emotional, vocational, and spiritual wellbeing have benefitted and the reduction in food and snack bills caused by smaller portions has been financially beneficial. God really does love us, and every aspect of our wellbeing, and He wants us to be well and whole—wellbeing in the fullest sense of the word."

REFLECT & RESPOND

Take a moment to go over some of the key topics from our look at how to live well physically, then consider how you could see an improvement in the following areas:

- Sleep: Are there any practical steps that you need to take to help you sleep better?
- Diet: Are there any changes you need to make concerning your current eating or drinking habits?
- Exercise: What one thing is a fresh motivation for you to exercise more regularly? What one change could you make to help you start or improve your exercise regimen?

LIVE WELL EMOTIONALLY

DAY 15

Emotional health matters

"But the fruit of the Spirit is love, joy, peace, patience, kindness, goodness, faithfulness, gentleness, self-control."

GALATIANS 5:22–23 (ESV)

If you had asked me a couple of years ago whether I thought emotional health mattered, I would have answered with an unequivocal "yes." If you had asked whether I was emotionally healthy, I would have given you a more qualified "yes." As I shared on Day 4, I was partly aware that the tiredness I was feeling was somehow related to the long haul of being involved in church leadership for over three decades. What I was less aware of was that there were some internal character issues that were contributing to this sense of depletion. Having done various personality profiles such as DISC, Myers-Briggs and the Enneagram,[1] I consistently come out as someone with a leadership gifting, drive, and the desire to achieve. However, as I began to read Peter Scazzero's *Emotionally Healthy Leader*[2] and looked more at my Enneagram "type," I started to become more aware of the "shadow side" of my strengths, such as a tendency towards drivenness and a fear of failure. This new self-awareness, along with regular input from my spiritual director and my Christian psychologist, has been fundamental to my more recent journey of increasing emotional freedom and wellbeing.

As I look back, I would not say that before this season I was emotionally unhealthy, I just wasn't as free as God had designed me to be. My emotional dial was probably sometimes on yellow. You may, however, be in a season when you are experiencing symptoms of depression or even burnout, and your emotional dial is firmly in the red. Wherever we're at emotionally, the good news is that God has a plan for our replenishment and thriving.

Before we delve into how to live well emotionally, it's worth making clear that our emotions really do matter. God Himself is an emotional being. Jesus, the Son of God, modeled this as someone who was and is intensely loving, sometimes joyful, sometimes righteously angry, and not afraid to cry. To be truly like Him, we may need His Spirit to touch and heal us to be able to fully and healthily express our emotions.

The humanity of Jesus highlights what psychologists have long recognized: that we have both "positive" and "negative" emotions, and there is a place for both. Barbara Fredrickson says: "Even the happiest people cry when they lose someone or something they cherish. They're angered by injustice and frightened by danger. Their stomachs turn when they see vomit or witness human atrocities."[3] The problem, however, is that we weren't designed to carry these so-called negative emotions long term, and too much negativity will overwhelm us and lead to burnout, as Elijah's experience in the desert so dramatically reveals. Rather, for our human flourishing, we need a significantly higher ratio of positive to negative emotions. Based on extensive research, Fredrickson recommends that we aim for a positivity ratio of 3:1. In other words, for every negative emotional experience that you endure, try to experience three positive ones. She describes this as "the tipping point, predicting whether people languish or flourish."[4] Some people have questioned Fredrickson's ratio, but it's widely acknowledged that positive emotions have been proven to have massive benefits in our lives: they help us feel good, broaden our outlook, build new skills, fuel resilience, and improve our physical health.

God of course knows all of this, because He designed us this way and He wants to help us and heal us emotionally. For me as a Christian, I am very grateful for the massive benefits of having the Spirit of God Himself living in me. For example, the more I develop my relationship with the Spirit, the more I experience the positive "fruit" of His presence in my life: "love, joy, peace, patience, kindness, goodness, faithfulness, gentleness, [and] self-control" (Galatians 5:22–23 ESV).

REFLECT & RESPOND

As we start this week, take some time to consider how you are doing emotionally. Take another look at your emotional dial and assess whether it's red, yellow, or green. If it's on red or yellow, begin to consider why. Invite the Holy Spirit to heal and help you grow and produce positive "fruit" in your life.

DAY 16

Freedom from fear

"There is no fear in love, but perfect love casts out fear."

1 JOHN 4:18 (ESV)

Yesterday we looked at how we all have the capacity for both positive and negative emotions. Today, let's look at how we can live free from a powerful (and often negative) emotion: fear. Although we briefly looked at living with a faith-not-fear mindset on Day 5, I'd like to revisit this topic of fear again because the presence or absence of fear has a huge impact on our emotional health.

It's important to recognize that not all fear is bad. Sometimes it is an appropriate response to a perceived threat or potentially dangerous situation that enables us to respond correctly, releasing adrenaline when we need it. When I talk about "fear" here, I'm referring to the type of fear that prevents us from living the life God wants for us, either by stealing our peace or by becoming a prison we can't break free from.

The five most common fears of people are reported as follows: the fear of heights (acrophobia), the fear of public speaking (glossophobia), the fear of snakes (ophidiophobia), the fear of flying (aerophobia), and the fear of spiders (arachnophobia). While occasionally I need to overcome nerves when speaking in public and I don't particularly like snakes or spiders, I wouldn't say I have an actual phobia of any of these. In fact, I wouldn't consider myself a naturally timid or fearful person. But over the past couple of years, as I indicated previously, I have become more aware of a specific fear that has held me back from experiencing deeper levels of emotional wellness, which is the fear of failure. This self-awareness has been crucial. Most psychologists and counselors agree that the first step in getting free from any negative or limiting emotion is to be able to first identify it, and even better, put a name to it. Alongside this awareness, I've experienced a corresponding deepened knowledge of God's love for me, which has begun to set me free in ways I couldn't have imagined.

As we have already seen, the sudden onslaught of fear played a key role in Elijah's meltdown in 1 Kings 19. A simple but deadly threat from Jezebel caused this bold man of faith to run in fear for his life. What is encouraging, though, is that through God's replenishment plan, Elijah clearly got free from this fear, and his boldness returned. A few chapters later, for example, we find him going back and boldly confronting King Ahab for his sin and pronouncing God's judgment on Jezebel. These are not the actions of a man still crippled by fear. We don't know what part of God's restoration process—from the visit of the angel, to the encounter on Mount Horeb—was most instrumental in bringing this regained freedom from fear, but what's important is that Elijah did get free and his faith and boldness were restored.

Speaking of freedom from fear, here's a great testimony of a young woman who is part of our church:

> *"I grew up in a Christian household but suffered from anxiety and depression from age 11 to my late teens, hidden behind a very shy and smiley demeanor. It was crippling and prevented me from doing most normal things that a teenager can do, and I often felt trapped at home, watching my friends and loved ones live life without me. Everyday activities such as shopping, getting in a car, or going out to a restaurant were all way too much to handle, and the guilt of holding my family back often sent me down a further spiral. However, there came a point*

when I was asked to do something out of my comfort zone. Rather than backing out, I decided to just "do it afraid," saying this over and over as a silent prayer: "God, I give this to You—I can't carry this on my own." This was the pivotal moment in my faith. I realized that if I fully put my trust in God, I could do anything. The switch flipped. From that moment, my life was transformed from one that was heavy and one that didn't have a hope for the future, to seeing endless possibilities. Each day I stepped out of my comfort zone—it wasn't easy, and I did have to put a lot of work in—but God brought me out of the darkness and into the light. I never believed anyone who told me that there was hope, or who'd said I will get better, but I did. It was a very long journey and still something that I continue to work on and trust in God for, but with God in my life I know I have a purpose and that I am ultimately and fully loved."

What I, with a more subtle fear of failure, and this young woman living for years in the overwhelming grip of fear have in common is that we both experienced freedom as we encountered the love of God—our focus tomorrow!

REFLECT & RESPOND

Given how paralyzing and destructive fear can be for our emotional wellness, take a moment to come before God and ask Him to help you. You may also need a trusted friend or spiritual leader to pray with you. If you are aware of obvious fears, write them down. Think about the root of those fears: how and when did they take hold? Then ask the Lord to reveal fears that are less obvious. Bring all your fears to God and ask for Him to fill you with His perfect love which casts out fear (1 John 4:18).

DAY 17

"See what great love the Father has lavished on us, that we should be called children of God!"

1 JOHN 3:1

Beloved

Of all the wonderful truths concerning our new identity in Jesus (see Day 2), the most significant for me, particularly in recent years, has been a stronger revelation that I am deeply loved! Being loved by God is something that I have known and experienced ever since I became a Christian, but since the spring of 2017, an even deeper revelation of this has been key to me living well emotionally.

One of the things that the Holy Spirit used to get through to me was some devotional exercises from the book *Journey with Jesus*,[5] written by my spiritual director, Larry Warner. Here are the chapter titles:

> Week One: God loves you.
> Week Two: God really loves you.
> Week Three: God really, really loves you!

By the end of my three-week saturation in this truth, I began to experience more than ever before how much I am *deeply loved by God*. An added blessing was a reminder that my name, David, means "beloved." That's at the core of my new identity: I am beloved of

God. Thankfully, this is also true for all those who are children of God. Whatever your birth name, if you are born again, you are beloved by Jesus, the Beloved of God (see Ephesians 1:5–6; Colossians 3:12)!

This knowledge of being deeply loved by God is foundational for us if we are to grow emotionally, spiritually, and relationally. In a less obvious way, being reminded of God's love and care most likely played a part in Elijah's journey of emotional replenishment, too. Let me remind you that the very first thing God did for His exhausted servant in the desert was to send an angel to touch him, speak to him, and feed him (1 Kings 19:5–6). This supremely tender act was not just to minister to his vital physical needs, since in an earlier incident God had provided for these same needs through ravens (1 Kings 17:2–6). This time in the wilderness, He doesn't send him birds but an angel. Why? Because an angel is a personal messenger from God Himself. This touch—these words, this provision from God's own messenger—was a way of God showing Elijah that he was not forgotten or finished, but that he was dearly loved, beloved by God.

Although angels are real, and sometimes do still come to minister to people, we don't need to wait for an encounter with one to know that God really, really loves us. The normal ways in which God reveals His love to us, especially since Jesus came to earth, are:

- **Through the Word of God.** Throughout the Bible, there are amazing promises concerning God's love for us. Here are just a couple for you to ponder: "See what great love the Father has lavished on us, that we should be called children of God! And that is what we are!" (1 John 3:1). Then there's this passage, from *The Message* version of the Bible: "None of this fazes us because Jesus loves us. I'm absolutely convinced that nothing—nothing living or dead, angelic or demonic, today or tomorrow, high or low, thinkable or unthinkable—absolutely nothing can get between us and God's love because of the way that Jesus our Master has embraced us" (Romans 8:38–39).
- **Through the Holy Spirit.** When we receive Christ, God's love is "poured out into our hearts through the Holy Spirit" (Romans 5:5). This completely transforms us. Again, I love how *The Message* version explains this in Romans 8:15–17:

"This resurrection life you received from God is not a timid, grave-tending life. It's adventurously expectant, greeting God with a childlike 'What's next, Papa?' God's Spirit touches our spirits and confirms who we really are. We know who he is, and we know who we are: Father and children. And we know we are going to get what's coming to us—an unbelievable inheritance!"

- **Through other people.** As we'll see when we look a bit later at how to live well relationally, we were designed for close relationships and for spiritual community—a place where we can be truly known and fully loved. Significantly, in the apostle Paul's letter to the Ephesians, he prays that the Christians, "being rooted and established in love, may have power, *together with all the Lord's holy people*, to grasp how wide and long and high and deep is the love of Christ" (Ephesians 3:17–18, my italics). Growing in love and grasping the love of Christ is best experienced "together" with others.

REFLECT & RESPOND

I encourage you to take some time to ponder the wonderful truth that you are dearly loved by God. He loves you; He really loves you; He really, really loves you! You are His beloved. Slowly read and meditate on 1 John 3:1 and Romans 8:15–17.

DAY 18

"May the God of hope fill you with all joy and peace as you trust in him."

ROMANS 15:13

A hope that doesn't disappoint

One of the keys to emotional wellbeing is having hope. Viktor Frankl, a Holocaust survivor of Auschwitz and Dachau and author of *Man's Search for Meaning*, tells of how hope was the single most important factor in surviving the Nazi death camps—even more vital than physical health. He tells the story of one man who was convinced that they would be liberated by Christmas. This hope kept him alive and positive for months. However, when Christmas came and went and they weren't freed, he simply curled up and died. When a prisoner lost hope, said Frankl, "he lost his spiritual hold."[6]

Most psychologists would agree on hope's central importance. In *Positivity*, Barbara Fredrickson describes it like this: "Deep within the core of hope is the belief that things can change. No matter how awful or uncertain they are at the moment things can turn out better. Possibilities exist. Hope sustains you. It keeps you from collapsing into despair. It motivates you to tap into your own capabilities and inventiveness to turn things around. It inspires you to plan for a better future."[7]

One of the major benefits of hope is that it helps us deal with suffering, setbacks, and disappointments. We all face many disappointments in life. Maybe you're currently struggling to deal with a relationship that didn't turn out as you expected, a job or career path that has changed, or a dream that doesn't seem to have come to pass. It seems that one of the reasons for Elijah's emotional collapse was an acute sense of disappointment—that the victory on Mount Carmel didn't result in the whole nation, including the royal family, turning back to God. It seems as if Elijah's Plan A was different from God's. The Lord knew that the king and queen were not going to relent, so He had a longer-term plan to remove them. But in the short term, without this same perspective, Elijah felt overwhelmed by a crushing sense of disappointment. (This is evident from his twice-repeated lament to the Lord on Mount Horeb—see Day 25.) Having lost all hope, he laid down, never wanting to get up again. Once again, the ministry of the angel was vital. Significantly, the first words that the angel spoke to him were, "Get up ..." and then a second time, "get up"—and we read, "So he [Elijah] got up" (1 Kings 19:5–8). Although we don't know what was going on for Elijah emotionally at this point, the fact is that we don't see him lie down again in this way, feeling completely defeated and suicidal. Even if hope only started as a glimmer, the fact of the angel's intervention means that Elijah was able not only to get up physically, but he could "get up" again emotionally. Then, when he met God at Mount Horeb, his hope was more fully restored.

Back in 2004, I had the experience of having to deal with a significant sense of personal and collective disappointment. We had spent considerable time and money pursuing a planning application for a six-acre site to build a church building. I went into the planning committee meeting and, after some debate, the committee voted 4-3 against it. As I came out of the town hall feeling completely devastated and much aggrieved, I immediately sensed the Lord speaking to me, letting me know that this was His overruling of the situation. This hope, this belief in a better future, completely changed my perspective and emotional state. To cut a long story short, we decided to let go of that site and ended up finding another at a much better location, which was 12.5 acres (more than double the size of the first one), and we managed to gain the support of the local government officials—including, crucially, the Chief Executive of the City Council. When we went back to the planning committee the second time, we won the vote 9-0. Happy days!

That, for me, was a relatively quick turnaround. But there have been many other battles with disappointment that I've faced over the years when things haven't turned out as I'd hoped. One of the things I've been learning recently is how to deal more effectively with such disappointments, including the need to sometimes appropriately "mourn" any sense of loss before moving on.

Disappointment can overwhelm any one of us. Life is not perfect, and challenges abound. Very often in this life, as we come to God, He will break through and bring turnaround—in His way and in His timing. In this respect, I can have a greater basis for hope than Elijah did, since my whole faith is based on the present reality of the risen Jesus, who paid for my sins on the cross and rose triumphantly from the grave. So, even if I don't see things come good in this life, I have a sure and living hope that all will be put right when Jesus returns and raises me up with Him!

REFLECT & RESPOND

Be honest with God about any disappointments you have. Spend time with Him and put your trust in Him. Be prepared to mourn for any situations that you are still struggling to come to terms with. Ask the Lord to help and to heal you and give you fresh hope even in challenging circumstances. Encourage yourself with the fact that we have an eternal hope—that there is a day when Jesus will come back, when everything will be put right!

DAY 19

"Rejoice always,
pray continually,
give thanks in all
circumstances;
for this is God's
will for you in
Christ Jesus."

1 THESSALONIANS 5:16–18

Gratitude

Gratitude has long been recognized as an important part of a wholesome and healthy life. Epictetus, the Greek philosopher, said: "He is a wise man who does not grieve for the things he has not, but rejoices for those which he has." More importantly, the Bible also highlights the importance of rejoicing and thankfulness: "Rejoice always, pray continually, give thanks in all circumstances; for this is God's will for you in Christ Jesus" (1 Thessalonians 5:16–18).

Modern psychology has been catching up with the wisdom of the ancients in understanding the importance of gratitude for our wellbeing. Studies have shown having an attitude of gratitude helps our mental and physical health and increases our happiness by as much as 25%. I love how this author described the freedom that comes with gratitude: "By cultivating gratitude, we are free from envy over what we don't have or who we are not. It doesn't make life perfect, but with gratitude comes a realization that right now, in this moment, we have enough, we are enough."[8] Moreover, gratitude helps us savor the good things in life, which in turn enables us to enjoy them all over again!

It is not enough, however, to feel grateful. Rather, we need to learn to express our gratitude. One leading psychologist emphasizes the importance of "gratitude practices," ranging from gratitude letters to gratitude visits to writing down each night three things that went well and thinking about why they went well.[9] Somebody in our church said she developed the habit of thanking God for ten new things every evening before falling asleep. As she began to do this, she started to sleep better, became more aware of the presence of God and His goodness, and when she woke up, she found that she was less anxious about what was coming up that day.

The Bible has many exhortations to be grateful but focuses primarily on expressing our thanks to God our Creator and Savior. The Old Testament book of Psalms is full of this. Some, such as numbers 145–150, are packed with praise and thanksgiving. Others involve the psalmist directly reminding—even instructing—himself to be thankful, before listing reasons to be grateful to God: "Praise the LORD, my soul; all my inmost being, praise his holy name. Praise the LORD, my soul, and forget not all his benefits" (Psalm 103:1–2). Many others, however, are known as psalms of lament, when the psalmist expresses his pain and struggle to God with total honesty, before concluding with declarations of praise and thanksgiving. For example, Psalms 42–43 repeat this same refrain: "Why my soul, are you downcast? Why so disturbed within me? Put your hope in God, for I will yet praise him, my Savior and my God" (Psalms 42:5, 11; 43:5).

It's interesting, however, to note that the account of Elijah seems devoid of such expressions of praise. Both in the desert and on Mount Horeb, he seems fully able to express how downcast and disturbed he is feeling (see Day 25), which is a good thing, but he does not turn this into positive declarations of what God has done or will do.

By contrast, another biblical hero, the apostle Paul, displayed a remarkable attitude of gratitude. One of his letters to the Philippians (known sometimes as "the epistle of joy"), was written from prison and includes amazing exhortations like, "Rejoice in the Lord always. I will say it again: rejoice!" (Philippians 4:4). Moreover, Paul clearly lived what he preached. While in a prison in Philippi, he and his companion Silas, rather than complaining, spent the night praying and singing to God. God responded by sending an earthquake that shook the foundations of the prison, opened the doors, loosed their chains, and eventually led to the jailor and his family believing and being baptized! (You can read more about this in Acts 16:25–34.)

All of this highlights that gratitude expressed to God is glorifying to Him, but also very good for us—and is one of the primary keys to us experiencing positive emotions. This increases not just our emotional health, but our spiritual wellbeing too.

REFLECT & RESPOND

Think about some gratitude practices you could adopt. You might want to take some time to read Psalm 103 and look at the God-given "benefits" that the psalmist highlights. Consider writing your own list of what you're grateful to God for and express your thanks and praise to Him.

DAY 20

Slow down to be present

"Be still, and know that I am God."

PSALM 46:10 (ESV)

Over the next couple of days, as we have been doing throughout the week so far, we will be exploring practices that are not only vital for our emotional health but will also prepare us to live well spiritually (our upcoming focus). These are the need to slow down in order to be present, and the call to practice "Sabbath."

Slowing down is essential, but it can also be hard. Most of us live in a fast-paced, busy world, where we are constantly bombarded by distractions from many quarters, especially from our phones. This makes us particularly vulnerable to burnout if our identity is rooted in what we do rather than in who we are. As an example, I know that many people really struggled with fear and uncertainty during the enforced lockdown at the height of the coronavirus pandemic, and the significantly slowed pace of living that came with it. I heard of some people who were so fearful of not being busy and productive that they ended up making long lists of things to do so that they could fill the space—anything but slowing down! In his excellent book *The Ruthless Elimination of Hurry* (subtitled "How to stay emotionally healthy and spiritually alive in the chaos of the modern world"), John Mark Comer quotes from a dialogue between two Christian leaders. John Ortberg, feeling overwhelmed by pressure and busyness, sought the following advice from the philosopher and Christian teacher Dallas Willard:

"What do I need to do to become the me I want to be?" Dallas's reply was simple: "You must ruthlessly eliminate hurry from your life."[10]

This is not just great counsel to prevent an enforced slowdown or burnout that Comer and many others have experienced. Neither is it just applicable to more naturally driven and "hurried" personality types like me. Rather, it is an essential part of growing in emotional freedom and spiritual vitality. Going back to Ortberg's original question, slowing down is a part of us being able to truly become the authentic person that God has designed us to be. Why? Because it is only as we learn to slow down that we are also able to be present.

Being "present" is very much in vogue today, often linked to the term "mindfulness." The Christian approach to being mindful includes this call to be present to ourselves but is founded on something much deeper and ultimately more liberating, which is being present to the One who is always present to us. It is about learning, along with the psalmist to "Be still, and know that I am God" (Psalm 46:10), worded by another translation as, "Cease striving and know that I am God" (NASB). For me personally, this call to "be present" has been a crucial part of my recent wellbeing journey. One of the key practices that has helped me in this is what is sometimes called "The Prayer of Awareness" (or the "Prayer of Examen" or "Daily Examen"), developed by the sixteenth-century saint Ignatius of Loyola. It is based on Psalm 139:23–24: "Search me, God, and know my heart; test me and know my anxious thoughts. See if there is any offensive way in me and lead me in the way everlasting."

Although there are different versions of this prayer of awareness, I use these five basic steps:

- **Thanks.** I begin by recalling specific good things that I have recently experienced and take time to thank God for them.
- **Search.** I sensitize myself to the convicting work of the Holy Spirit by praying the

"search me" prayer, viewing this as an invitation to freedom. Very often I don't sense anything at this point, so I don't strive but trust that by praying this way the Lord can speak to me at any point during my day.

- **Review.** This is the heart of the prayer, where I look back over my previous day or time since my last Examen and review. Sometimes I find it helpful to ask myself: "Where have the interactions and circumstances of my life been taking me—toward God or away from God?"
- **Confess.** Then I ask God to forgive me for anything that I have become aware of in Steps 2 and 3, being careful not to allow any feelings of condemnation, but rather to receive God's forgiveness and experience His love.
- **Abide.** Finally, I acknowledge that I cannot live a God-honoring life alone, but I need His abiding presence and an ever-deepening internalization of His love for me and of His power working within me (see Ephesians 3:16–19).

I often pray this awareness prayer first thing in the morning and use it to center myself on the Lord and His presence, often journaling at the same time. Occasionally I use it in the middle of the day or early evening when I can reflect back on what's happened over the previous few hours or day, inviting God to speak to me about where I've either met with Him or missed Him in the opportunities and challenges of my daily life. Using this prayer regularly helps me become more aware of where I am at emotionally, and of how the Lord wants me to grow spiritually.

REFLECT & RESPOND

Why not begin to experiment by praying this prayer or elements of it a couple of times a day? As you do, know that the Lord loves to answer this prayer. As you grow in self-awareness, it will not only help you emotionally but also spiritually—our next focus.

DAY 21

"The Sabbath was made for man, not man for the Sabbath."

MARK 2:27

Sabbath

Before we finish our focus on living well emotionally and get ready to look at living well spiritually, today we reflect on something that is of huge benefit for both. It is the much misunderstood and often-neglected concept of the Sabbath (meaning to "stop or cease"). The Sabbath principle goes right back to the account of creation in the book of Genesis, where we read of God working for six days and resting for one, taking time to delight in all that He had made. This creational principle of resting, delighting, and then working from rest became established as a pattern for God's people in the Ten Commandments. It's worth noting that this fifth commandment, that no "work" shall be done one day in seven, is the most detailed of all the commandments (see Exodus 20:8–11). It became a key part of the distinctive faith of the people of Israel, and something that the Old Testament prophets regularly reminded them to honor: a day set aside for worship and rest, with obvious physical benefits for those working on the land, as well as a time to recharge emotionally, spiritually and relationally.

By the time of Jesus, sadly some in the religious establishment had made the Sabbath an unhelpfully restrictive religious duty. Without undermining the need for a Sabbath, Jesus sought to redress the balance, encapsulated by a simple phrase: "The Sabbath was made for man, not man for the Sabbath" (Mark 2:27). In other words, the Sabbath, the principle of one day of rest in seven, is a gift from the Creator to His creation. Sabbath has been given to us for our good and is vital for our weekly rhythm of replenishment.

Sabbath is not something to be viewed as a burden but as "an invitation to delight ... the best day of our lives."[11] Sabbath is not just a time to "stop" for one day a week; rather, "it's a spirit of restfulness that comes from abiding, from living in the Father's loving presence all week long."[12]

When we rest, delight, and worship on the Sabbath, and embrace that for which it was designed, it affects the rest of our week. As the Old Testament scholar Walter Brueggemann put it: "People who keep sabbath, live all seven days differently."[13]

I find all these perspectives to be really helpful ways of thinking about Sabbath. Right from my earliest days as a Christian, I started intentionally observing a proper day off each week and was immediately aware of its benefits. In college, when I first became a Christian, I very quickly decided that on Sundays I would not do any studying—even before important exams. Since being involved in church work, I have had to shift my Sabbath away from a Sunday for obvious reasons, but I've kept the principle of a weekly Sabbath, enjoying at least 24 hours without work. There are countless times when I have gone into a Sabbath feeling very tired, but come out feeling very refreshed—physically, emotionally, spiritually, and often relationally, too.

In addition to weekly Sabbaths, it's important that we have other breaks or holidays (Old English: "holy days") during our year. The biblical year is full of feasts and festivals not just for the purpose of worship and celebrating the Lord's goodness, but also because of their replenishing effect on us.

Let me conclude with a reminder of the purpose of the Sabbath: "In six days the LORD made the heavens and the earth, and on the seventh day he rested and was refreshed" (Exodus 31:17). If the Creator of the universe takes a day off, how much more do we need to take Sabbaths to rest and be refreshed!

REFLECT & RESPOND

Do you take a weekly Sabbath? Are there any adjustments that you could make? Consider how you could get household jobs done before your day off. Given that the purpose of the Sabbath is rest and replenishment, think about a few key things that you can do on your Sabbath (such as sleeping longer, enjoying extended time with God, having a special meal, spending time with close family and friends, enjoying nature, or doing other things that refresh you).

LIVE WELL SPIRITUALLY

DAY 22

"Whoever drinks the water I give them will never thirst."

JOHN 4:14

True rest and refreshing

Have you ever gone on a much-needed break or vacation, only to come back feeling just as tired—anything but rested and refreshed? One of the reasons is that although vacations can be good and even essential for our physical and emotional replenishment, they don't necessarily satisfy something even deeper, which is our need for spiritual rest and replenishment.

In recent years, at a time of considerable departure from established religion in much of the Western world, there has been a corresponding rise of interest in spirituality and spiritual experience. This spiritual hunger is not something new. Back in the fifth century, Saint Augustine famously said: "You [Lord] have made us for yourself, and ***our hearts are restless, until they can find rest in you***" (my italics). Many authors have sought to describe this human condition. Crusade for World Revival founder Selwyn Hughes wrote:

> *"God has built into us a desire for relationship with Him, which if not satisfied leaves us open and*

> *vulnerable to other sources of satisfaction. If God is not satisfying our souls, we will seek something else to satisfy us. This is where our problems begin... This desire for relationship with God is described in the Bible by many words—desire, hunger, longings, but perhaps the most descriptive of these words is thirst."* [1]

Ruth Haley Barton takes it a stage further:

> *"There is an even greater truth: before you were even aware of your desire for God, God desired you. He created you with a desire for him that groans and yearns in the very fiber of your being."* [2]

The importance of our spiritual relationship with God is emphasized throughout the Bible. For example, in 1 Thessalonians 5:23, the apostle Paul talks about God's plan for us to be whole and holy in every area of our lives, and sets this out in the following order: "spirit, soul and body." Notice how he mentions our spirit first, then our soul (mind, will, and emotions), then our body. Even though when it comes to our replenishment God often starts with the physical (which we've already covered), it is clear that our spiritual wellbeing is of critical and central importance to every other area of our lives.

For much of my childhood and adolescence, even though I had a loving family and lots going for me, I was increasingly aware—especially during my teens—that something was fundamentally missing from my life. I had what some describe as "a God-shaped hole," which included a sense of inner restlessness. But then, at the age of 19, I finally decided to pray and ask Jesus to come into my life. Not only did I experience a tremendous sense of being forgiven and made new on the inside, but I was filled with God's presence, satisfying me in the depths of my being in a way that I had never known before. For the first time in my whole life, I felt deeply at rest and truly refreshed. The even better news is that this experience continues to this day!

This is not something unique to me but is something that is available to all who accept what Jesus is offering them. While our individual experiences may vary, the promise of the Bible is that all who believe in and receive Jesus are born again, made spiritually new and alive through His resurrection power. We are given the gift of His

Holy Spirit, who fills us with the love and presence of God Himself (see John 3:5–7; Ephesians 2:1–6; 1 Peter 1:3–4). It's only then that our spiritual thirst truly begins to be satisfied, as "a spring of water welling up to eternal life" (John 4:14).

However, once we are born again and have this well within us, we still need to "drink" regularly. We need to keep coming to Christ, spending time with Him, and allowing the presence of the Holy Spirit to fill and refill us daily (see John 7:37–39). Why? Because in the words of the twentieth-century church leader John Wimber, "we leak!"

For the next few days, we'll explore how we can fill and keep refilling our spiritual tank.

REFLECT & RESPOND

Pause and consider your spiritual wellness. If you've never experienced Jesus coming into your life, then why not invite Him to do so today? (The prayer in at the end of the book will help you.) If you have been born again, thank Him for the wonderful privilege of being a child of God, and of having His Spirit within you. Then, ask the Lord to fill and refill you with His presence. Pray for a season of fresh encounters with the presence of the living God.

DAY 23

"Come near to God and he will come near to you."

JAMES 4:8

Spiritual renewal

It's only happened to me once. I was driving along the highway around the city where I live, and as I came to an exit ramp, my engine suddenly ground to a halt. … I had run out of gas. However, while this may have been an isolated incident, there have been plenty of times when I have allowed my fuel gauge to get into the red zone—something which I've only recently discovered is not only risky but ultimately can damage the engine. (You can tell I have a thing with gasoline and cars!) So I'm trying to do better and keep my fuel tank more regularly topped off. The same principle applies to my spiritual life. If I don't pay regular attention to the dial on my dashboard and regularly seek to refill my spiritual tank, I will start getting depleted on the inside, causing damage not just to the spiritual area of my life, but to every other part as well.

It seems clear that Elijah hit rock bottom, not just physically and emotionally, but spiritually, too. This mighty man of faith and prayer, who saw great miracles and experienced great victories in the name of the Lord, came to a point in the desert where he felt completely spiritually defeated and depleted. It's not clear exactly why. But from the evidence of the rest of Scripture and the experience of Christians throughout history, I want to tentatively suggest that the combination of physical exhaustion and emotional depletion may have had the effect of draining him spiritually too. I know from personal experience that tiredness in other areas can have a negative impact on my spiritual health.

Furthermore, the intense spiritual warfare Elijah experienced at Mount Carmel may have left him initially "high," and then vulnerable to a spiritual low—especially due to the well-timed missile of fear fired by Jezebel. (From talking to many people over the years, a time for us to be especially alert is after a positive spiritual encounter or blessing.) Elijah may have been giving out, without sufficiently receiving from the Lord for himself. This is certainly something that many leaders can testify is a cause of spiritual burnout.

The good news is that God didn't leave Elijah spiritually depleted. Instead, He began to lovingly restore him, first through the ministry of the angel and then by a personal encounter with His presence. This required a 40-day journey from the desert near Beersheba through the wilderness to Mount Sinai (called Mount Horeb in 1 Kings 19). It was on this mountain where, centuries earlier, God had appeared to Moses, revealed His glory, and given him the Ten Commandments (you can read more about this in Exodus 19–20).

So how does this apply to us today as we consider our own spiritual replenishment and wellness? First, and foremost, like Elijah, by learning to seek the Lord. When my daughters were still young, I remember playing hide-and-seek with them. Although in reality I was always available for them, there was something about the thrill of seeking and finding me that was all part of the game. In some ways, there are similarities when it comes to us seeking God. While He is always present and available, it sometimes seems as if He deliberately hides Himself from us, so that we can seek Him and find Him in a deeper way.

In particular, the Lord desires us to spend time alone with Him. This call to solitude and being in the presence of God is not the same as isolation. Rather, solitude—spending time alone with someone who knows and loves us completely—is absolutely central to our spiritual walk.

Theologian Henri Nouwen wrote: "Without solitude it is virtually impossible to live a spiritual life. ... We don't take the spiritual life seriously if we do not set aside some time to be with God and listen to him."[3] The greatest example of this is Jesus Himself, who throughout His earthly ministry prioritized time alone with God (see Mark 1:35; 6:46; Luke 4:42). If we want to become His disciples, we need to imitate His example, knowing that we have His promise: "Seek and you will find" (Luke 11:9).

Jesus isn't just our example, but also our mediator. Since we are living after His death, resurrection, ascension, and the outpouring of the Holy Spirit, we don't have to wait, like Elijah did, to go on a 40-day pilgrimage to a holy mountain in order to meet with God. Rather, in Jesus, God has come to be with us—and through the new birth and the infilling of the Holy Spirit, as Christians we have the Lord's presence inside us (see 1 Corinthians 3:16; 6:19 and Colossians 1:27). This is an amazing reminder of the huge benefits we have, even more so than the powerfully anointed Old Testament prophets like Elijah. This means, in the words of the seventeenth-century believer Brother Lawrence, we can learn to "practice the presence of God" in the ebb and flow of our daily lives. In the language of the New Testament, it's not so much that we need to pray, "God, please be with me," but, "help me be more aware of the reality of Your presence in and with me all of the time."

REFLECT & RESPOND

Take some time today to thank God for His presence. Invite Him to help you be more aware of Him in your everyday life. Then begin to consider spending more time in your daily, weekly, and annual schedule to seek out the Lord, taking encouragement from the exhortation in James 4:8.

DAY 24

A two-way conversation

"And pray in the Spirit on all occasions with all kinds of prayers and requests."

EPHESIANS 6:18

Yesterday we reflected on the wonderful reality that through Jesus and through His Spirit, God comes to live inside of us. We also established that we need to play our part if we are to enjoy spiritual renewal by spending time alone with Him in worship and prayer. Today, let's look at a key component of this relationship, which is being secure enough in God's love for us that we can be truly honest before Him.

Elijah is a good example of this. Although he was living under the Old Covenant (as laid out in the Law of Moses), he was still unafraid to be open and honest in his dialogue with God. In 1 Kings 17 and the early part of 1 Kings 19, we've already seen him express his honest faith and anguish in the raising of the widow from Zarephath's son and, by contrast, his expression of utter despair in the desert. As we move through chapter 19, we see him being similarly authentic in his encounter with the Lord at Mount Horeb.

Notice that God takes the initiative, simply asking Elijah twice the same question: "What are you doing here, Elijah?" (1 Kings 19:9, 13). When an all-knowing God asks a question, it is not because He doesn't know the answer; it's because He's seeking to engage us in an honest conversation. He is a relational God and knows that we, like Elijah, can lose perspective. He loves us and has a plan for our wellbeing. Author Jeff Lucas imagines God posing this question as an invitation, something a bit like this: "Elijah. Talk to me! Throw aside your nice, pleasant speech and just tell me, what's going on in that locked mind of yours."[4]

Then, notice that Elijah is clearly not afraid to speak his mind to God. Twice he replies: "I have been very zealous for the LORD God Almighty. The Israelites have rejected your covenant, torn down your altars, and put your prophets to death with the sword. I am the only one left, and now they are trying to kill me too" (1 Kings 19:10, 14). The fact that he repeats himself highlights that he is stuck in this mindset. As is often the case with us, Elijah's statements are a mixture of truth, half-truth, and falsehoods. But they also reveal that he feels safe enough and close enough to God that he can be totally honest with Him. He's not trying to dress up his situation or present things in an overly religious way: he is just telling God how he feels about things—even if he is misguided and even if there is an absence of the positive turnaround to praise that we see in many of the psalms of lament (see Day 19).

If Elijah could feel secure enough with God to be this honest, how much more can we today when we have the fuller revelation of God through Jesus Christ! Christian prayer is not a ritual or a religious duty but a dynamic relationship with a triune God, Father, Son, and Holy Spirit.

First, Christian prayer is talking to God your Father. When Jesus was teaching His disciples to pray, with the helpful template of what we now call the Lord's Prayer, He taught them to begin by addressing God as "Our Father in heaven." It is an invitation to authentic relationship. Church leader Nicky Gumbel explains it: "[God] is our loving Father and we have the extraordinary privilege of being able to come into his presence and call him 'Abba'—the Aramaic word for which the nearest translation is 'Daddy' or 'Dear Father.' There is remarkable intimacy about our relationship with God and about praying to our Father in Heaven."[5] Since God is not only "our Father" but also "in heaven," we can pray with intimacy and honesty but also with awe and confidence because we are praying to the holy, all-powerful Creator Himself, with and for whom nothing is impossible.

Second, Christian prayer is through the Son. We have no right to stand before God on our own behalf, but because of Jesus and His sacrifice for us, we have open access to the presence of God Himself (see Hebrews 10:19). He has made the way for us to come to Him with boldness, praying in the authority of the name of Jesus.

Third, Christian prayer is by the Spirit. It's great to be reminded that we are not left alone to struggle in our prayers. Rather, God, by His Spirit has come to live inside us. One of the many wonderful ways that the Spirit strengthens us is by helping us to pray (see Romans 8:26–27; Ephesians 6:18).

There's nothing like having a two-way conversation with this amazing God!

REFLECT & RESPOND

I hope that you're inspired by Elijah and his faith-filled but honest relationship with God. Take some time to consider how honest you're being with God in your life right now. Are there any areas in your life that you are internalizing by yourself, or are talking about with other people but not with God? Bring those things to the Lord and speak freely and honestly. Then spend a few minutes thanking God the Father, Son, and Holy Spirit for the privilege of being able to pray whenever and wherever you are.

DAY 25

"We do not know what we ought to pray for, but the Spirit himself intercedes for us."

ROMANS 8:26

God's not in a box!

One of the keys to true, ongoing spiritual renewal and wellness is to realize that God is not someone we can put in a box. He is the Sovereign Creator and He wants to reveal Himself in new and creative ways—not necessarily how we expect Him to!

When I first became a Christian, my prayer life tended to be very active—I loved to walk and pray—and it tended to be fairly loud, too! During this season, the main way I learned to pray was using the Lord's Prayer.[6] Rather than simply reciting it in a few seconds, I found huge benefit in approaching this prayer as a topical outline. As I learned to pray each phrase at a time, interacting with the Holy Spirit and allowing Him to lead me, I found myself growing in a deeper relationship with the Father.

Over the years, while continuing with the foundation of the Lord's Prayer, I have learned that God is a God of great variety and there are many ways to meet with Him. More recently, I've begun to discover new pathways that have helped me realize new things about myself and experience God in a new way—especially through times of contemplation, stillness, and through the prayer of self-awareness we have already explored (see Day 20). In addition, I have found increased strength in using the set prayers and Scripture readings from the daily prayers of the Church of England. And there are plenty of other ways I'm yet to discover!

We see something of this same creativity in the way that God revealed Himself to Elijah on Mount Horeb. Elijah was obviously used to hearing the word of the Lord and seeing God display Himself in great power. He was no doubt familiar with the dramatic ways that God had previously displayed Himself to Moses on that same mountain centuries earlier. Here, though, in 1 Kings 19, He instructs Elijah to get ready, for "the LORD is about to pass by," and arranges for the coming of a mighty wind, an earthquake, and fire. This time, however, it is made clear that: "the LORD was not in the wind ... the LORD was not in the earthquake ... the LORD was not in the fire' (19:11–12). It's as if God was saying, "Elijah, don't put me in a box. You've known me as a God of great power, of signs and wonders, but in your state of depletion, I want to reveal myself to you in a different way." In very telling language, the passage concludes, "after the fire came a ***gentle whisper***" (19:12, my italics)—a still, small voice, or a sound close to silence (see Day 27 for more on this).

Before we conclude today's study, let me summarize for you some of the different pathways that you might find helpful in developing your relationship with God:

- Read and reflect on Scripture: Expect God to speak to you (see Day 26).
- Journal: Write down your reflections from your daily experiences and your time in the Bible, recording what you sense the Lord is saying to you.
- Pray the Lord's Prayer: Taking a phrase at a time as a guide.
- Pray other prayers that are recorded in the Bible: Consider the Old Testament Prayer of Jabez (1 Chronicles 4:10) and the New Testament prayers of the apostle Paul (Ephesians 1:17–19; 3:16–19).
- Pray in the Holy Spirit: Reread passages about the role of the Spirit (Romans 8:26–27; 1Corinthians 14:14–15; Ephesians 6:18).
- Sing worship songs to God: There are many great resources to aid you in this.
- Pray the Prayer of Awareness, or "Examen" (see Day 20).
- Pray set prayers or "offices," such as the daily prayers of the Church of England.[7]

- Spend time in solitude and silence: Learning to be still, pausing to either meditate on Scripture or just bask in God's loving presence.

REFLECT & RESPOND

In light of this, take some time to consider your relationship with God. What are the primary ways that you can connect with Him? Without neglecting these in any way, look again at the list above and consider whether the Lord may be wanting to help you encounter Him in different ways.

DAY 26

Listen and learn

"So faith comes from hearing, and hearing through the word of Christ."

ROMANS 10:17 (ESV)

If we are to live well spiritually, we must learn not only to speak to the Lord in worship and prayer but also to listen to Him. Today and tomorrow, I want to look at the two primary ways that God speaks to us. The first foundational way is through the Bible. The apostle Paul emphasizes the importance of this in his letter to his disciple Timothy by reminding him: "All Scripture is God-breathed and is useful for teaching, rebuking, correcting, and training in righteousness, so that the servant of God may be thoroughly equipped for every good work" (2 Timothy 3:16–17). Notice here the claim that all Scripture, the whole of the Bible, is inspired by God. This means that when we read the Bible, we are reading not just the words of human writers, but the Word of God (see 2 Peter 1:20–21).

Therefore, reading and reflecting on the Bible is a primary means of us getting to know God and His ways. An Old Testament hero like Elijah would probably only have had access to what is known as the Torah (the first five books of the Bible). But even then, his whole revelation of God as Yahweh—the God of

Israel—and his understanding of what God was calling him to do, was clearly shaped by this recorded and passed down revelation. How much more can our worldview be positively shaped by renewing our minds when we have not just the complete Old Testament but the New Testament, through which we get a fuller revelation of God, in and through His Son, Jesus Christ.

In addition to us gaining a more general revelation of God through the Scriptures, I, like many other Christians throughout the ages, have found God speaking to me personally, as I regularly read and meditate on His Word devotionally. I particularly love the example of the great Christian philanthropist George Müller:

> *"I saw more clearly than ever that the first great and primary business to which I ought to attend every day was to have my soul happy in the Lord. The first thing to be concerned about was not how much I might serve the Lord, how I might glorify the Lord; but how I might get my soul into a happy state, and how my inner man might be nourished. ... I saw the most important thing I had to do was to give myself to the reading of the Word of God and to meditation on it, that thus my heart may be comforted, encouraged, warned, reproved, instructed; and that thus, whilst meditating, my heart might be brought into experimental communion with the Lord. I began therefore to meditate on the Word of God; searching, as it were, into every verse, to get blessings out of it. ... The result is ... that by breakfast time, with rare exceptions, I am in a peaceful if not happy state of heart."*[8]

Notice the link here between meditation on Scriptures and spiritual health.

So how do we read and meditate on the Word "devotionally"? Here are a couple of practical ways that I would recommend, one modern and one ancient.

The first is the principle of SOAP, taught by Pastor Wayne Cordeiro in his book *The Divine Mentor.*[9] I first read this in 2009 and have found this simple acrostic helpful:

S: Scripture: Deliberately pause on a verse or passage
O: Observation: Ask questions about what it's saying
A: Application: Consider how this Scripture applies to you
P: Pray: Talk to God in the light of what you sense Him saying to you

The second is the ancient practice of *lectio divina*, which means "divine reading." Developed in the sixth century by Benedict of Nursia, *lectio* is still widely used and endorsed today. The following quote from Pope Benedict emphasizes its usefulness: "I would like to mention the spread of the ancient practice of Lectio Divina or 'spiritual reading' of Sacred Scripture. It consists in pouring over a biblical text for some time, reading it and rereading it, as it were, 'ruminating' on it as the Fathers say and squeezing from it, so to speak, all its 'juice,' so that it may nourish meditation and contemplation and, like water, succeed in irrigating life itself."[10] The practice of *lectio* is made up of four similar but slightly different elements to SOAP:

- Read (*lectio*): Deliberately focus on a specific passage, verse, or phrase, and read and re-read it several times, allowing the Lord to highlight a key truth to you.
- Meditate (*meditatio*): Combining the disciplines of observation and application, consider what God is saying to you through the passage. I usually like to journal about this, which helps me to slow down and consider more fully what I am sensing, as well as to keep a record for me to go back over.

- Pray (*oratorio*): Allow your whole being to become prayer, honestly expressing your deepest thoughts, feelings, and desires to God.
- Contemplate (*contemplatio*): Gently let go of all thoughts and feelings and rest with gratitude for what God has given you.

In summary, as we take time to immerse ourselves in the truths of the Bible on a regular basis, our values are shaped and our minds are renewed to who God is and how we are to relate to Him and to others. Through devotionally reading and reflecting on specific portions of Scripture, God speaks to us personally, by His Spirit.

REFLECT & RESPOND

If you are not already regularly reading the Bible, then I encourage you to explore some of the resources available to help you. You could visit YouVersion.com and download a Bible reading plan, or have a look at some Bible reading apps. *The Bible* with Nicky and Pippa Gumbel is one that many people find particularly helpful. As you read the Bible, try out the steps I've suggested today. Record what you sense the Lord might be saying to you today.

DAY 27

The still, small voice

"For God alone, O my soul, wait in silence, for my hope is from him."

PSALM 62:5 (ESV)

One of the great gifts of the Christian life is that we can know God personally, and we can grow in hearing Him speak to us. Jesus put it simply: "My sheep listen to my voice; I know them, and they follow me" (John 10:27). As a young Christian I knew that this was true, but I had a hard time discerning God's voice—often confused as to whether what I was hearing was from the Lord or myself! However, the more I immersed myself in the Bible, the more I became confident in recognizing God's voice. Much of my confusion dissipated when I realized that I was unlikely to hear God's voice audibly—it was more that the God who had come to live inside me wanted to communicate to me, to my spirit, by His Spirit. He wants to do the same for you, too!

In that respect, we are in a much more privileged position than those who lived in Old Testament times when the people of Israel had to rely on God speaking to them through specially anointed servants, known as prophets. Elijah was one of the most influential of these, and throughout his ministry we see him being supernaturally gifted to know what God was saying and to speak on His behalf. While prophets and the gift of prophecy do exist in the New Testament era, they function differently—by that point, those who are children of God have the Spirit living within them and can hear Him speaking to them. Our responsibility is to learn to listen to Him.

One of the keys to listening to God is to cultivate the spiritual discipline of silence. In fact, it has often been helpfully pointed out that an anagram of "listen" is "silent." Silence is not just external but internal: "Silence is the ceasing from words and inward striving. It begins as an outward discipline, but the goal is that it would become an inward reality. As you begin to be silent, you will discover the tremendous amount of noise ('unsilence') that you carry with you in your heart and mind."[11] I don't know about you, but I find this "true silence" a considerable challenge. It takes real intention and discipline. John Mark Comer's way of describing internal noise really resonates with me: a "wild beast in desperate need of taming," with "no off switch."[12]

This is where silence is linked to the other spiritual disciplines of slowing down, Sabbath, and solitude, which are all essential if we are ever going to learn to be truly silent. Silence both externally and internally is critical if we're going to grow in truly listening to God: "The journey of silence is a journey toward internal silence that will help you to hear the still small voice of God and to be more readily aware of what is stirring within you."[13] This reference to the still, small voice of God refers back to Elijah's encounter with the Lord at Mount Horeb, when God spoke to Him through "a gentle whisper" (1 Kings 19:12).

This still, small voice or gentle whisper is the primary way that God still speaks to people today. It means that we don't have to go looking for outward signs or an audible voice (these very occasionally happen). Instead, we can learn to sense the quiet promptings of the Holy Spirit who dwells within.

Sometimes we can struggle to hear Him because we haven't yet learned to discern this still, small voice. At other times it's because God may have spoken to us, but we haven't been listening.

Jeff Lucas highlights this point in reflecting on the Lord's dialogue with Elijah:

> *"Perhaps we don't hear Him more because we are looking for Him to say something new, when actually He may well be bringing us back to a previous statement that we've ignored or disobeyed. Certainly, this was Elijah's experience. Once out of the cave, cloak wrapped around his face for fear that he might actually see Yahweh, it's question time again: 'What are you doing here, Elijah?' Same old question. Back to square one. Sometimes we feel as if God has gone silent on us. Perhaps it's good to check to make sure that last time He spoke, we heard and responded."* [14]

REFLECT & RESPOND

Take some time now to be silent. Find a quiet space if you can. Let yourself relax, handing over any distracting thoughts to God. As you still yourself, quietly welcome His presence. Enjoy and linger in this for a while. Notice if He is saying anything. If not, don't worry—just enjoy His company.[15]

DAY 28

Desire, discipline, delight

"Delight yourself in the LORD, and he will give you the desires of your heart."

PSALM 37:4 (ESV)

These three words changed my life! I was a relatively new Christian with a longing to know God better, and I heard someone describe the progression that we normally go through in our relationship with the Lord as a journey of desire, into discipline and into delight.

Let me unpack this a bit:

1. **Desire.** This relates to what we looked at on Day 22: that we have a strong longing, a deep need, a great thirst for God. That has certainly been the case in my experience since I became a Christian. But desire alone won't lead to spiritual satisfaction and wellbeing. Rather, we need to embrace ...
2. **Discipline.** This is where the rubber meets the road! If the key to our spiritual wellness is our relationship with God, and if our spiritual health impacts every other area of our lives, then we need to be disciplined as well as spontaneous in our development of this relationship. Just as discipline helps us grow in other areas of life, so spiritual disciplines help us grow spiritually. As

we have now seen, these include living a life of thanksgiving, slowing down, being present, celebrating the Sabbath, praying, reading the Bible, practicing solitude and silence, and learning to listen to the voice of the Spirit. As ever, Jesus is our supreme example in these things. I remember studying His earthly life and ministry when I first became a Christian and being struck by how He regularly withdrew to lonely places to spend time alone with His Father and came back freshly filled with wisdom and strength. As we follow His example, there are three things for us to focus on:

- Find the **time**: Although we can meet with God at any time, there is something about setting aside a particular time to meet with Him. Choose the time of the day when you are at your best and try to be consistent with it.
- Find the **place**: Again, because God is always with us, we can meet with Him anywhere. However, there is something about finding a place or places where you will be undisturbed and where you can meet Him in a more intimate way. For me, my favorite daily meeting places are my study or out walking. (For longer times, I often go to a retreat center.) I know others who meet with God early in the morning in a coffee shop! Find what works best for you.
- Find the **way**: There are many ways you can meet with the Lord and develop your relationship with Him, but here are two foundational pathways. First, spend time listening to Him by regularly (daily if you can) reading and reflecting on portions of the Bible and allowing His Spirit to speak to you. Second, speak to Him in worship and in prayer. In addition to these personal disciplines, it's vital for us to include a regular rhythm of meeting with other Christians in larger and smaller settings, where we can worship, learn, and grow together. It's important, however, to realize that spiritual disciplines, while vital, are not an end in themselves. Rather, like a trellis for a vine or a climbing plant, which provides stability and structure with the goal of producing great grapes or beautiful flowers, so spiritual disciplines provide consistency in our walk with God, enabling us to produce the fruit of a Spirit-filled life. The more we embrace discipline in our walk with the Lord, the more we will experience ...

3. **Delight.** "Delight yourself in the LORD, and he will give you the desires of your heart" (Psalm 37:4 ESV). Our seeking will lead to finding—as God increasingly reveals Himself to us, satisfying our deep spiritual thirst in a way that only He can.

This continual, even daily, progression from desire to discipline to delight will help you grow spiritually whether you are exploring faith, are new to the faith, or are a mature believer—whether you are spiritually empty or spiritually full!

REFLECT & RESPOND

Take some time to reconsider your spiritual life. Think about this as a key dial on your dashboard and assess whether you feel spiritually full (green), empty (red), or somewhere in between (yellow). Take a look again at the call to find a time, a place, and a way, and begin to think about how you can start to increase spiritual disciplines in your life.

LIVE WELL RELATIONALLY

DAY 29

"The LORD God said, 'It is not good for the man to be alone.'"

GENESIS 2:18

Relationships matter!

As I look back on my life, one thing has become really clear to me: relationships matter ... a lot. I can't count the number of times I've opened up to close companions—be it my wife, friends, mentors, or close colleagues—and having shared my struggles with these trusted people, I've come away feeling healthier, lighter, clearer, and more positive because of their empathetic listening, prayer support, and godly counsel. This need for close, healthy relationships is something common to us all.

As a psychologist friend of mine recently said: "There is a healing power in relationships." In fact, the vast majority of his clinical work is taken up with helping people deal with the mental and emotional turmoil caused by relational difficulties with others.

So why do relationships matter so much? The simple but profound truth is that we are hard-wired as human beings to need one another, designed at the core of who we are for giving to and receiving from other people. The human brain, more than that of any other species, is designed for relationships—so much so that some neuroscientists have called it the "social organ." Unsurprisingly, then, researchers have found that the factor distinguishing the happiest 10% of people from everyone else was the strength of their social relationships.[1] This is, in part, physiological: "When we make positive social connections, our body releases oxytocin—a pleasure-inducing chemical—into our bloodstream. Oxytocin is sometimes referred to as 'the love drug,' as it plays a role in bonding. ... Furthermore, oxytocin also reduces our anxiety, improves our concentration and focus, and helps to regulate our cardiovascular system."[2] This positive relational connectivity helps us in the different seasons of life. It is most often through our relationships with others that we survive life's lowest moments and toughest challenges. Friendships lift, encourage and enrich us.

The importance of relationships is central to God's plan for our thriving. The Bible teaches that not only is relational connection God's idea, but God Himself is a relational being. The Christian doctrine of the Trinity highlights that there is one God, eternally existing in the three "persons" of the Father, the Son, and the Holy Spirit. At the heart of this divine community is eternal love and concern for each other. Since God is at His core a relational being, so are we. Made in His image (see Genesis 1:27), we are designed to live in community, loving and caring for one another. This means that while we have "vertical" needs that can only be satisfied by a close, personal relationship with God Himself, we also have "horizontal" needs that can only be met by healthy relationships with other people.

So, as we look at how to live well relationally, we are going to be considering two key issues. One is the presence or absence of meaningful relationships. Since relationship with others is so central to our whole existence as human beings, we need to consider whether we have enough of the right kind of relational connections and whether we are sufficiently investing in those relationships.

The other is the relative peace of our existing relationships. At the heart of biblical wellbeing or "peace"—both Old Testament ***shalom*** and New Testament *eirene*—is relational harmony and unity, first with God and then with others. Just as there is nothing like relational harmony to increase our overall sense of wellness, so there is nothing like relational discord to negatively impact every other area of our lives.

REFLECT & RESPOND

Consider your relational dial. Think about specific people in your life. Who do you love being with? Who energizes you? Consider how you could further the relationships that you find to be the most life-giving.

DAY 30

Not good to be alone

"Two are better than one."

ECCLESIASTES 4:9

One of the greatest problems we are facing today, and one that you may be experiencing personally, is that of loneliness. This has a hugely negative impact on our overall health and wellbeing. Loneliness and poor social connections are thought to be as bad for your health as smoking 15 cigarettes a day and can increase your risk of death by as much as 29 percent.[3] Research also shows that lonely people are more likely to suffer from dementia, heart disease, and depression.

God's simple declaration at the creation of the first human being was this: "It is not good for the man to be alone" (Genesis 2:18). His solution? He created "another," a woman to be united to and have a deep and intimate relationship with the man. Although this is a wonderful passage celebrating the origins of marriage, it has a much broader application than that. It highlights that as human beings, whether we are single or married, introverts or extroverts, we were not designed to be alone.

Loneliness is not only about how many people we are connected to but about the quality of those connections. The problem is that we don't always end up making the right choices when it comes to meeting this relational need. In *The Power of the Other*, Henry Cloud describes how we, like mobile phones searching for a connection, have an inbuilt need to connect with other human beings. In practice, however, we usually end up in one of four "corners" or places of connection, the first three being negative. First, there is the place of *No Connection*, when either through circumstance or choice we fail to be "emotionally and functionally invested in other people, in a give-and-receive dynamic." Second, there is the place of *Bad Connection*: "not necessarily a connection with a bad or abusive person, although it may be. Instead, it is a connection, preoccupation, or pull toward a person who has the effect of making you feel bad or 'not good enough' in some way." Third, there is the place of *Pseudo-Good Connection*, which can seductively make us feel good, "temporarily and superficially making one feel better" without meeting our deepest needs. Finally, there is the place of *True Connection*, where "you can be your whole self, the real, authentic you, a relationship to which you can bring your heart, mind, soul and passion. Both parties to the relationship are wholly present, known, understood, and mutually invested. What each truly thinks, feels, believes, fears, and needs can be shared safely."[4]

The human need for true connection with others is clearly illustrated in the story of Elijah. One of the most salient lessons of his burnout in 1 Kings 19 is that prior to going into the desert, Elijah dismissed his servant, the only companion he had at that critical point in his life. This was a big mistake. At this point in his story, more than ever, Elijah needed friends. I love how Jeff Lucas describes the effect this must have had: "[Elijah] tried to carry a huge load upon his shoulders single-handedly—and like a champion weightlifter, who manages for a while to hold up an impossible burden, his arms shaking with strain, blood vessels and veins popping out on his blood-filled face, he suddenly snapped."[5] Why? Because he was firmly in the first corner of *No Connection*.

Thankfully, God had a plan for Elijah's relational wellbeing. First, because Elijah was in a desert and there were no other human beings out there, God directly intervened by sending His angel to him. Later, at Mount Horeb, God gave him a more permanent solution by telling him to go and seek out a young man called Elisha. This was a hugely significant turning point. For the first part of his ministry, due to persecution from the royal family, Elijah carried out his prophetic ministry largely alone. Now, the Lord in His kindness provided him not just with a co-worker and future successor, but a companion who from then until his death would be alongside him.

We all need others to help us, not just in times of crisis, but in every season of our lives. As we saw in the Introduction, it's a popular Bible reading to include in wedding services, but Ecclesiastes 4:9–12 is for all of us: "Two are better than one, because they have a good return for their labor: if either of them falls down, one can help the other up. But pity anyone who falls and has no one to help them up. Also, if two lie down together, they will keep warm. But how can one keep warm alone? Though one may be overpowered, two can defend themselves. A cord of three strands is not quickly broken."

Put simply, we need each other.

REFLECT & RESPOND

Have another think about Cloud's four corners of connection. Consider which most accurately describes where you're at right now. Then re-read the verses from Ecclesiastes 4, and ask the Lord to help you develop healthy, life-giving relationships.

DAY 31

"For where two or three gather in my name, there am I with them."

MATTHEW 18:20

Levels of connection

In the last two days, we have established that we are wired for relational connection. So how do we develop healthy relationships?

First, we need to be clear that not all our relationships are or should be on the same level. Cultural anthropologist Edward Hall suggests that we have four spaces of relational proximity: an intimate space reserved for close friends and family; a personal space used for conversations with friends, associates, and group discussions; a social space reserved for strangers, newly formed groups, and acquaintances; and a public space used for speeches, lectures, and theater.[6] This principle of various circles of connection is illustrated, with some nuances, in the life of Jesus Himself. He had some very clear circles of relationship:

- The **three**: Jesus had a close-knit inner core of disciples, Peter, James, and John. Significantly, He only took these three with Him to the high moment of being transfigured on the mountain and to the low point of feeling utterly overwhelmed in the Garden of Gethsemane.

In addition to these three, it seems as if he had another inner core, the family of Lazarus, Martha, and Mary.

- The **twelve**: This group of disciples also included the inner core of Peter, James, and John. The New Testament makes clear that while "the twelve" were called to Jesus to learn and continue His ministry after His ascension, the first reason was "that they might be with him" (Mark 3:14).
- The **72**: A wider group of leaders who Jesus involved in His ministry.
- The **crowds**: The people who Jesus ministered to through His preaching, teaching, and healing.

Jesus not only had these different levels of relationships, but He clearly balanced His community time with the groups of three and twelve, and His giving out in ministry to the crowds.

The great news for us is that Jesus not only modeled the need for community, but He set up a community that we could all be a part of: the Church. While not everyone has the privilege of a close, healthy, nuclear family, all of us can discover and develop community within the context of a local church. Contrary to some people's misperception, the Church is not a building. Neither is it primarily an organization, but it's the family of God, the Body of Christ, and is central to God's eternal master plan not just for our needs but for the wellbeing of the entire human race. The Church operates on essentially two levels. There is the universal Church, which spans the ages and the continents. Every born-again Christian is part of this much bigger company. However, every Christian will flourish if they can also belong to a local church, as modeled by the local churches mentioned in the New Testament.

I remember the first time I started connecting with a local church in my early years as a Christian and the huge blessing it was to me. Whenever I started feeling spiritually and emotionally low or felt tempted to miss an early morning communion service or mid-week small group gathering, I would try to push on through anyway—and would always come away from those meetings strengthened as time and again the Lord met me in a special way. This appreciation of being part of a church—even though I now lead one(!)—has continued for many years: from the joy of worshiping God in unison with many to the openness and accountability of sharing honestly and praying together with a few. I wholeheartedly concur with Pastor Rick Warren here: "Being included in God's family is the highest honor and the greatest privilege you will ever receive. Nothing ever comes close. Whenever you feel unimportant, unloved, or insecure, remember to whom you belong. ... While your relationship to Christ is personal, God never intends it to be private. In God's family you are connected to every other believer, and we will belong to each other for eternity."[7]

The great news is that being part of the Church not only enables us to belong but also to develop different levels of relational connection. We see this in the Early Church. After the day of Pentecost, the believers gathered regularly in both small and large settings, from house to house and in the temple courts (see Acts 2:46; 5:42). Today, churches across the world have discovered the importance of a similar pattern: smaller group contexts where mutual sharing and support can happen at a deeper level, and larger gatherings where whole congregations can meet for the purpose of public worship, teaching, ministry, and evangelism.

REFLECT & RESPOND

Look again at Jesus' circles of connection and begin to consider who is, or could be, in your core group of relationships. Take time to thank God for key people in your life and pray that He would bless them as they have blessed you. If you are not part of a local church or actively committed to one, or you're in a church but not part of a small group, I encourage you to join!

DAY 32

"How good and pleasant it is when God's people live together in unity!"

PSALM 133:1

Growing in relational health

Yesterday we looked at the importance of having different levels of relational connection. Today we're going to be looking at understanding how we can invest in relationships that most contribute to our relational health, without neglecting those who appropriately need our care.

In *People Fuel*, Dr. John Townsend paints a picture of seven categories (or C's) of relationships:[8]

- **Coaches**: life coaches, mentors, spiritual directors, therapists, or trainers
- **Comrades**: a life team who, like a family, are joined together for mutual growth and support
- **Casuals**: low-commitment but enjoyable relationships
- **Colleagues**: work associates who create a meaningful transfer of relational nutrients in the cause of a common task
- **Care**: relationships in which you are providing good for those who need your support

- **Chronics**: people who are a significant ongoing drain on you, with no real change in sight.
- **Contaminants**: people who are intentionally seeking to bring you harm

In his experience, Townsend has found that most people "don't have a sufficient number of coaches, comrades, and even casuals for health and success, and at the same time, they feel burdened by the amount of time they spend giving to individuals, chronics, and contaminants. This leads to exhaustion, lack of energy, problems in priority and clarity, and lack of effectiveness."[9] His advice is to start by adding in the top three energizing groups, so as to gain confidence in reassessing the bottom three, before making an important caveat that we mustn't see care relationships as a problem: "it is the time, energy, and resources that you don't have available which are the problem."

So, how do we prioritize and develop energizing and life-giving relationships? First, we need to invest time. In the case of Elijah and Elisha, for example, it seems likely that they were in close proximity for a whole decade. So by the time of Elijah's departure to heaven, their bond of friendship and affection had grown strong, as evidenced by Elisha's repeated protest: "As surely as the LORD lives and as you live, I will not leave you" (2 Kings 2:2, 4, 6). This was not just because he wanted to receive a double portion of Elijah's anointing, but because of a genuine love and loyalty to his friend and mentor. Similarly, as Elijah went up to heaven, Elisha cried out, "My father! My father!" (2 Kings 2:12), clearly indicating that he felt he was losing someone who had been like a father to him. Such relationships are built over time and require genuine love and authenticity to flourish and deepen—whether in the context of marriage, family, or friendship.

Second, the best relationships require vulnerability: "The capacity to be vulnerable allows us to truly know each other, to support each other, and to be a source of life and energy for each other. People who do not have several vulnerable relationships often struggle with isolation, energy problems, and self-doubt."[10] We see examples of vulnerability all through the Bible, but our foremost example of this is again Jesus Himself. In almost direct contrast to Elijah, who dismissed his servant at the point of his greatest need, Jesus deliberately called Peter, James, and John to be with Him in His darkest hour of trial and showed that He was fully able to share with them His inner angst and need for their support: "My soul is overwhelmed with sorrow to the point of death. Stay here and keep watch with me" (Matthew 26:38). Notice here that He is not with the crowds, not even with the twelve, but with His inner core of three. If Jesus needed to be vulnerable in this way, then so must we!

Third, we need to set appropriate boundaries. As we have seen, not all relationships are good for us, and even good ones need appropriate limits if they are to remain helpful. Since we each only have a finite amount of time and energy, we must learn to set proper boundaries. It's been said that the only people who will have an issue with you establishing boundaries are those who benefitted from you not having any! Despite being interruptible, approachable, and endlessly kind, even Jesus had clear boundaries. It's OK to draw a line somewhere.[11]

REFLECT & RESPOND

What changes might you need to make in terms of time, vulnerability, or the setting of boundaries in your relationships? Once you have considered this, write down the most significant take-home point for you as it relates to your relationships.

DAY 33

Loving others

"Since God so loved us, we also ought to love one another."

1 JOHN 4:11

For the first ten years of our marriage, Karen and I had some great times but some tough times too. Part of the struggle was the simple fact that we were two independent and often selfish people learning to become "one." Another key factor was that both of us brought "baggage" from our past, especially from before we became Christians. However, one of the fundamental problems was that even after ten years we still didn't fully "get" one another! That began to change when we went on The Marriage Course[12] and discovered, in particular, that we each had different "love languages" (a principle developed by Dr. Gary Chapman).[13] My primary love language is words of affirmation, while Karen's is acts of service.

This helped us start to make sense of some of our struggles. I would occasionally express feelings of being "unloved" because Karen didn't verbally express love very often, and she would reply in exasperation, "How can you think I don't love you when I wash your socks and underwear week in and week out?" Similarly, when I would say "I love you" quite frequently, she would be thinking, *If you really loved me you would remember to take the trash out!* Twenty-five years later, while we're still on a journey, our relationship is so much deeper and richer because we've learned to focus on each other's needs and not just on our own.

This principle of putting others first applies to all relationships, whether in marriage, family, or friendship. For those of us who are Christians, we have the advantage of both the example of Jesus Christ, the most loving and unselfish person who ever lived, and, through His sacrifice for us, the means of receiving the extravagant love of God the Father (see Day 17). As we grow in knowing how deeply loved we are by God, so we can grow in really loving others. The apostle John put it this way: "This is love: not that we loved God, but that he loved us and sent his Son as an atoning sacrifice for our sins. Dear friends, since God so loved us, we also ought to love one another" (1 John 4:10–11).

So how can we love others better? There is so much that could be said but based on the expert advice of Dr. John Townsend,[14] I want to highlight a few practical areas:

Be present

One of the greatest gifts we can give people is our presence. Rick Warren puts it this way, in the context of marriage, but with broader application: "The most desired gift of love is ... focused attention. Love concentrates so intently on another that you forget yourself at that moment. Attention says, 'I value you enough to give you my most precious asset—my time.' Whenever you give your time, you are making a sacrifice, and sacrifice is the essence of love."[15] Central to this is offering the gift of affirming, non-judgmental listening. The famous psychologist Sigmund Freud famously said, "Fifty percent of my patients get better without me saying anything." In other words, they talked; he listened; they got better. You don't have to be a trained psychologist to offer a listening ear. If being a good listener is not something that comes naturally to you, you may have to work at it. Learning not to interrupt or not to immediately give advice is a discipline and a skill worth cultivating.

Be positive

There is huge power in giving and receiving genuine, specific affirmation and encouragement. Proverbs 12:18 says: "The words of the reckless pierce like swords, but the tongue of the wise brings healing." When our daughters were younger, while Karen and I sometimes needed to correct and discipline them, we primarily sought to fill their lives with words of love, affection, and praise. It works just the same in our adult relationships—whether it be in marriage, at work, in church, or with other friends.

Be honest

When we have built a genuine platform of acceptance and positivity, we can give feedback. Proverbs 27:6 says, "Faithful are the wounds of a friend" (ESV). One of the reasons we need to be prepared to give and receive honest, constructive feedback is because we all have blind spots, and we need others to help us see what we can't currently see! Having others in our lives is key to not just relational connectivity, but to growing in emotional freedom and Christlikeness—which is true freedom.

Give wise counsel

One of the greatest gifts we can give and receive from each other is Holy Spirit-inspired wise counsel. Proverbs 15:22 aptly puts it this way: "Plans fail for lack of counsel, but with many advisors they succeed." Whether on a personal level or in a work context, I'm hugely grateful for the countless occasions when wise counsel from my wife, mentors, or colleagues has helped shape the course of my life and steered me onto better paths.

REFLECT & RESPOND

Why not look at these four areas—being present, being positive, being honest, and giving wise counsel—and consider which you most need to grow in? Consider whether there's something practical you can do to serve a friend or family member (maybe sending a gift or an encouraging message). Then ask the Lord to fill you with His love and wisdom and to empower you to become a better friend to those around you.

DAY 34

"Forgive us our sins, as we have forgiven those who sin against us."

MATTHEW 6:12 (NLT)

The journey of forgiveness

If we want to live well relationally, we not only need to increase our true connection through proximity, vulnerability, and love, but we need to be prepared to guard our relationships. Sometimes, because of the inherent frailty of human relationships, this will involve going on a journey of forgiveness.

Unsurprisingly, studies have shown that forgiveness improves mental health and relational quality, as well as increasing self-esteem and lowering anxiety and depression. It can even impact our physical health.

I remember many years ago an incident concerning a woman who had a problem with her neck and had to wear a brace for it. She came forward in a church meeting in response to an invitation to forgive people who had hurt her. When she sat back down, someone sitting behind called her name. She turned around and found that her neck was completely healed! This doesn't of course mean that all sickness is related to unforgiveness, but it does highlight how forgiveness, and the ability to let go, can have a huge impact on our physical, emotional, spiritual, and relational wellbeing.

The Bible has a lot to say about the importance of

forgiveness. Right at the heart of the Lord's Prayer is the phrase, "forgive us our sins, as we have forgiven those who sin against us" (Matthew 6:12). This is so important that it's the one line of the prayer that is also re-emphasized at the end. Our unwillingness to forgive can have a devastating impact on our relationship with God, as well as on ourselves, leaving us in a place of torment. When left unresolved, unforgiveness can easily lead to a root of bitterness which not only harms us but those around us (see Matthew 18:21–35; Hebrews 12:15).

However, God has provided for us so that we don't have to stay imprisoned by unforgiveness or bitterness. Because of what Jesus has done, we can receive and release forgiveness. The apostle Paul puts it this way: "Get rid of all bitterness, rage and anger, brawling and slander, along with every form of malice. Be kind and compassionate to one another, ***forgiving each other, just as in Christ God forgave you***" (Ephesians 4:31–33, my italics). This doesn't mean that forgiveness is necessarily easy—especially if we've been deeply hurt and the sense of injustice is huge. But it does mean that through Christ it's possible—and essential. As we choose to forgive, sometimes freedom comes immediately. On other occasions, forgiveness opens the door for a healing process to begin. Similarly, forgiveness doesn't necessarily mean that trust will be immediately sufficient for reconciliation to take place (or is always appropriate, as in the case of abuse, for example—see Day 35), but it does pave the way for the journey to begin.

The important thing is that we actively apply ourselves to forgiveness and relational restoration. As we do, it will have huge beneficial effects not just on our relationships, but on our whole sense of thriving. And since relational harmony is at the heart of God's will for His people, walking in unity attracts His commanded blessing (see Psalm 133).

Another important thing to consider is how we can learn to become people who are less easily offended in the first place. Elijah is a great example of this. Having been instrumental in the blessing and physical salvation of the widow from Zarephath and her family, he suddenly finds himself being blamed by this woman for the death of her son. Remarkably, Elijah shows no sign of resentment at this unjust accusation. Rather, because of his love and compassion, he positively acts to bless her and sees her son raised from the dead. He then hands the son back to the widow without any semblance of pride or self-justification (see 1 Kings 17:17–24). The simple lesson from this is that the more we grow, the more loving and the less easily offended we can become.

It's inevitable in any human relationship that from time to time we will disagree, annoy one another, hurt one another, and potentially separate from one another. But great relationships are those where through love, persistence, and character, we are prepared to work things out and move on. In fact, as we weather these relational storms, our connections come out strengthened on the other side.

REFLECT & RESPOND

It might be challenging, but it's important to spend some time reflecting on any areas of unforgiveness or bitterness that you may have. If you become aware of a person or people that you need to forgive, ask God to first forgive you for holding an offense. Then, choose to begin the journey of forgiving the other person. As you start to let go of the unforgiveness, invite the Lord to heal and to help you.[16]

DAY 35

Reconciliation

"As far as it depends on you, live at peace with everyone."

ROMANS 12:18

As we saw yesterday, forgiveness is an essential part of living well emotionally. However, it is only the first of our steps towards something greater: relational reconciliation.

I remember seeing the impact of this in a young woman's life many years ago. She had completed an Alpha Course,[17] became a Christian, and received the greatest reconciliation of all—between her and God, her heavenly Father—yet continued to struggle in her relationship with her stepfather and over the absence of her birth father, whom she hadn't seen since she was three years old. After a time of growing in her faith, she felt God prompting her to write a letter to her estranged father. This brought an immediate release, helping her to get free from the rejection she had experienced. Soon she felt able to forgive her father and to let go of unresolved anger towards him, resulting in what she described as "the greatest release ever." The following week was her birthday and, to her amazement, she received a letter from him. They decided to meet up. She said: "I went alone to meet him. ... He hugged me when he met me and it all felt right. I finally had a 'dad's hug.' ... He told me that he loved me, that he had always loved me." A few years later, with the relationship restored, she wrote: "All feelings of rejection are gone and I love the fact that God dealt with this, and I have been able to move forward into the life he has destined for me!"

This highlights how initiating reconciliation, especially with those close to us, can bring release and restoration to all concerned. In one of his New Testament letters, the apostle Paul instructs: "If it is possible, as far as it depends on you, live at peace with everyone" (Romans 12:18). However, as this verse implies, relational reconciliation isn't always possible. That may be because the other person is not interested in reconciliation. There are also some cases when attempting to reconcile is inadvisable, such as when a person has been abused and the abuser shows no signs of changing their behavior. In particularly painful situations, it's important to get help and healing and to go on a journey of forgiveness, while also putting up clear boundaries.

One of my favorite examples of reconciliation is the Old Testament character Joseph, son of Jacob. You can find his story in the closing chapters of the book of Genesis. In summary, as a young man of 17, Joseph was physically and emotionally abused by his brothers, nearly killed, thrown into a pit, and sold into slavery. After 13 years in Egypt, most of them spent unjustly in prison, Joseph was spectacularly promoted to second-in-command to Pharaoh. As well as being used by God to save multitudes of Egyptians from famine, Joseph was also able to save his family, thus ensuring the future survival of the people of Israel. The high point of the drama was when Joseph, having secretly watched his brother's remorse and repentance at what they had done to him, and having been able to forgive them, reveals himself to them in an act of beautiful reconciliation. Many years later, the brothers came to him afraid that this may not last. Joseph's response is not just a fitting end to the story, but an appropriate end to our week on relational wellbeing: "'Don't be afraid. Am I in the place of God? You intended to harm me, but God intended it for good to accomplish what is now being done, the saving of many lives. ...' And he reassured them and spoke kindly to them" (Genesis 50:19–21).

I remember studying this story many years ago and noting a number of key wisdom principles in approaching this important but sensitive subject of reconciliation:[18]

Be reconciled to the right people. It's interesting to note that we only see Joseph being reconciled with his brothers—those close to him who had a common understanding of the Lord as their God—rather than others (such as the slave traders) who had also mistreated him. Without over-generalizing from this one specific example, it does highlight, as we've already seen, that we need to be careful and prayerful in who we are to undertake reconciliation with.

Be reconciled at the right time. Joseph deliberately didn't press for reconciliation the moment he saw his brothers reappear before him in Egypt. Rather, he waited for two long years, probably in order to see genuine repentance on the part of those who had offended him. Sometimes, when the issue is relatively minor, it is best to seek reconciliation fairly quickly, rather than letting an issue fester. But when the offense is major, and particularly where there is no evidence of repentance, it is best to proceed with caution.

Be reconciled in the right context. Eventually, when Joseph did make himself known to his brothers and confronted them for their sin against him, he did so in person, and in private—something particularly important for us to take note of today when so much is unwisely and hastily shared online.

Be reconciled with the right attitude. Significantly, by the time Joseph revealed himself to his brothers, he seems to have been in a place where he was free from bitterness and revenge. He was secure in the knowledge that God had overruled even their great sin to bring ultimate good, and that he, Joseph, was concerned for their wellbeing. It's a remarkable example and it highlights that we need to go on a journey of forgiveness (see Day 34) to get our hearts right if we are to experience true and lasting reconciliation.

REFLECT & RESPOND

As you consider this important but potentially very challenging issue of relational reconciliation, consider whether there's anyone you need to be reconciled to. If so, you may want to relook at the four principles I've just outlined. As you move forward, pray that God will turn harmful situations into good, just as He did for Joseph. If you're unsure how to proceed, talk things through with a wise and trusted friend or mentor.

LIVE WELL FINANCIALLY

DAY 36

"The earth is the LORD's, and everything in it."

PSALM 24:1

Stewardship, not ownership

It may partly have been due to my religious upbringing. It may partly have been due to my not being especially bothered about money or possessions as I grew up. But shortly after I became a Christian, I remember being slightly puzzled (even vaguely annoyed) when I started hearing people talk about finances in the context of faith. My reasoning was that following Jesus was primarily about my internal life, especially my spiritual development, so I struggled to see why money was particularly relevant.

However, the more I studied the Bible, the more I came to see that our attitude towards money and the material world is of considerable importance. Jesus Himself talked a lot about money: 16 of the 38 parables were concerned with how to handle money and possessions. In the gospels (Matthew, Mark, Luke, and John), an amazing one out of ten verses (288 in all) deal directly with the subject of money. Moreover, if we return to the biblical root word for "peace," *shalom*, we see that true wellbeing includes the financial or material area of our lives. Throughout the Bible, God is revealed as the Creator of the material universe and also One who is lovingly active as the provider in all areas of our lives. He is interested in our material needs and has the best plan for our financial lives, which includes our being provided for.

This is such an important topic, not least because a lack of financial peace has a huge impact on other areas of our lives. For example, money worries are one of the main causes of stress, often causing marital and relational strain. The Stress in America 2023 Survey reports that nearly 40% of adults "feel consumed by worries regarding money." Among American parents, that number jumps to 66%. And nearly one in three adults identified money as "a cause of fights in their family."[1]

Instead of huge financial anxiety and stress, imagine living in financial peace: having margin each month, with opportunities to save for the future and to give to help others in need. For the rest of this week, we will look at key principles and practices to help turn this dream into a reality. Today, I want to briefly look at something that is foundational to living well financially, which is "stewardship" (or "management"). This is critical because we don't live with financial margin and peace by accident but by intentionally managing our money well. From the beginning of the Bible, we see the first human beings given the gift and responsibility of enjoying and stewarding God's creation. Sadly, since the Fall, we have an inbuilt human tendency to live independently of our Creator, viewing our lives, our money, and our possessions as our own. Thankfully, however, through Jesus, God has redeemed us and restored us to a right relationship with Himself. Those of us who follow Jesus are to renew our minds to a new perspective, seeing that everything we are and everything we have ultimately comes from God. Our part is to steward all that He has given us.

Embracing stewardship over ownership starts with taking responsibility for our lives: "You are not your own; you were bought at a price" (1 Corinthians 6:19–20). Once we accept that we ourselves belong to God, we can move on to embrace the fact that so does everything else that we have. As the Psalms declare: "The earth is the LORD's, and everything in it, the world, and all who live in it" (Psalm 24:1).

Celebrating the fact that God is the owner of everything—and that we are His stewards—is crucial if we are to start enjoying internal freedom from fear and worry. A stewardship perspective is foundational for us to begin to experience financial peace.

Once we have settled that God is the owner, we can begin to learn how to manage our finances His way—and His ways are best!

REFLECT & RESPOND

Think about the financial dial on your dashboard, and consider whether it's on red, yellow, or green. How might knowing God is the owner and you are His steward help you thrive financially?

DAY 37

God's plan for our financial wellbeing

"But seek first his kingdom and his righteousness, and all these things will be given to you as well."

MATTHEW 6:33

Yesterday we looked at the foundational principle of stewardship. Over the next few days, we'll be looking at some key practices essential for managing our money well: focusing particularly on spending carefully, saving wisely, and giving generously. Before we get into these practicalities, I'd like to first address another perspective, which is vital if we're to be financially free. This concerns us getting the right biblical balance on this whole subject. Imagine there's a highway called "God's Plan for Your Financial Thriving," and on either side are two ditches: "Poverty Perspective" and a "Materialistic Mindset."

A poverty perspective views life through the lens of scarcity and is often accompanied by a fear of lack. So how do we begin to get free from this? Yesterday we saw that true *shalom* means "wellbeing in every area of life," including financial and material provision. In Genesis 2, right at the beginning of the Bible, we see the Lord putting the first human beings in the Garden of Eden, providing for their every need. The consistent theme throughout the Old Testament—even after the Fall—is that God provides for His people. This becomes even clearer in the New Testament as we see that God is our heavenly Father, who wants to provide for our basic needs and free us from fear and worry (see Matthew 6:25–33).

A materialistic mindset is where we become excessively concerned with physical comforts or with the acquisition of wealth and material possessions. This applies regardless of one's income. People with lower incomes may have a materialistic mindset, while people with higher incomes can be very fearful of lacking anything (even if this is more a matter of perception than reality). The root of this is putting our trust in money or possessions rather than in God. In order to get free from a materialistic mindset, we need to begin by recognizing the truth of Jesus' teaching that "life does not consist in an abundance of possessions" (Luke 12:15), whatever the rest of the world tells us. In the Sermon on the Mount, Jesus invites us to "seek first the kingdom of God and his righteousness, and all these things will be added to you" (Matthew 6:33, ESV). Simply, it's a matter of priorities and focus: seeking first God's kingdom and the things He values helps free us from materialism, and believing the promise of God's provision addresses any fear of lack.

When we're in God's will, seeking first His kingdom, we can enjoy His peace and expect His provision even when economic circumstances look bleak. This is wonderfully demonstrated throughout the story of Elijah, which is set against the backdrop of the three-year drought. God was in no way limited by this situation. First, at the Kerith Ravine, the Lord saw to it that: "ravens brought [Elijah] bread and meat in the morning and bread and meat in the evening, and he drank from the brook" (1 Kings 17:6). When the brook dried up, God then sent Elijah to a widow, miraculously supplying both his and her family's needs (see Day 40). Finally, God provided for his exhausted prophet in the desert by bringing bread and water through an angel (see Day 11).

Many of us may not experience quite so dire a financial or material situation as Elijah, and we won't necessarily need ravens or angels to bring us bread or see our food supernaturally multiplied (though I have heard of this happening). However, we can know God as our provider and trust Him for His provision in every season of our lives.

In 1988, Karen and I sensed the call of God to start a church in the city of Peterborough. Even though we knew we were putting God's kingdom first, it didn't make it easy. We were raising a young family and about to live on one very modest salary; house prices were on the rise and we ended up buying almost the cheapest house in the city. We took out a low-start mortgage, which meant that the payments started low and quickly went very high. All of this meant that we soon had insufficient money coming in just to pay our basic bills, but we decided to close the door to debt by committing not to borrow anything apart from our mortgage. Because we were doing God's work and were obedient in putting Him first in our giving (see Day 40), we felt able to pray with confidence that He would provide. And He did! Month after month we experienced supernatural provision. Sometimes it was larger amounts from known sources, at other times it was small amounts anonymously given. On one occasion we were so hard-pressed that Karen didn't have enough money for formula for our baby daughter. As she was praying in the kitchen, she heard an envelope drop on the mat in our living room. She opened it up and there, in cash, was the exact amount she needed. We were in the will of God and God kept on providing!

Since then, we've had many opportunities to trust God both personally and in leading the church. Many years later, we needed millions of pounds to buy land and build a large building in Peterborough, but the faith we needed for this wasn't any greater than we'd needed for our daughter's milk. We've learned that when we are in the will of God, we can expect the provision of God.

REFLECT & RESPOND

Think about the picture of the highway and the two ditches. Are you someone more prone to a poverty perspective, a materialist mindset, or a combination of both? Re-read Matthew 6:33 and consider how Jesus' teaching can and will set you free.

DAY 38

"I have learned to be content whatever the circumstances."

PHILIPPIANS 4:11

Cultivating contentment

Integral to living out God's plan for our financial health is the need for us to manage the resources we've been given—whether they're large or small—so that we end up with margin. Financial margin means that instead of living beyond our means or just up to our means, we live within our means.

One of the most common reasons we don't have financial margin is that we're not content with where we're at and what we've got. This means that it's possible for us to be in a relatively affluent nation—perhaps even relatively well-off within that context—and still feel that we need more. Often this desire for more is not based on what we need but on what we want, not helped by the pressures of our consumer culture, the constant onslaught of advertising, and our tendency to compare ourselves to others. We think we need more and therefore spend more, often beyond our means. A primary way to get free from unchecked consumerism is to cultivate contentment.

If we look at the example of Elijah, he seems to have been generally content with God's provision for his life. There's no sign, for example, of him moaning at the seeming boredom of living in Kerith and being fed a diet of bread and meat every day! But perhaps the best biblical example of contentment, apart from Jesus Himself, is the apostle Paul. Listen to his remarkable words in Philippians 4:11–13: "I have learned to be content whatever the circumstances. I know what it is to be in need, and I know what it is to have plenty. I have learned the secret of being content in any and every situation, whether well fed or hungry, whether living in plenty or in want. I can do all this through him who gives me strength." In 1 Timothy 6:6–10, warning of the dangers of materialism and an ever-increasing desire to get richer, he emphasizes again the power of being content:

> *"But godliness with contentment is great gain. For we brought nothing into this world, and we can take nothing out of it. But if we have food and clothing, we will be content with that. Those who want to get rich fall into temptation and a trap and into many foolish and harmful desires that plunge people into ruin and destruction. For the love of money is a root of all kinds of evil. Some people, eager for money, have wandered from the faith and pierced themselves with many griefs."*

This striking passage highlights the dangers of greed and the blessings of contentment. Growing in contentment is a very effective antidote to any tendencies we have to overspend.

There's a lot that we could say about the importance of controlling our spending, but here are a few simple suggestions that you might find helpful:

- Assess where you're at financially. If you're regularly spending more than your income, then know by how much.
- Develop a budget, or at least a clear idea of what you can reasonably afford to spend in any given week or month, and don't exceed it.
- Do everything you can to get out and stay out of debt. Financing our lifestyle with debt is a very short-term and dangerous strategy. If you're in debt, know the terms and interest rates. Don't be embarrassed to seek advice and get a debt-reduction

program together to help you begin to pay off your debts, starting with those that have the highest interest payments. (Help with getting out of debt is available.[2])

- Avoid impulse spending. Try not to spend as soon as you see something online or in a store—especially if it's a significant purchase. Take time to "cool down" and prayerfully ask God to guide you. If in doubt, don't buy it! I know friends who never make a major purchase in the moment and will always leave it 24 hours before deciding—especially if the salesperson is telling them that the deal is only available that day.
- Cultivate a habit of thankfulness for what you do have rather than focusing on what you don't have.

If you begin to let contentment rather than covetousness shape your spending, you can start to live below your means and get some financial margin, which is a key part of living well financially.

REFLECT & RESPOND

As you think about your finances, consider how you can cultivate a greater sense of contentment. Then look again at the suggestions on controlling your spending on the previous page. Choose one area to start working on, as a first step to getting greater margin in your own finances.

DAY 39

Save and give

"A generous person will prosper; whoever refreshes others will be refreshed."

PROVERBS 11:25

The eighteenth-century preacher John Wesley famously said: "Earn all you can, give all you can, save all you can." We might not be surprised by the call to give and even to save but notice Wesley's first encouragement is to earn. We will be exploring the theme of work in the context of living well vocationally in a few days. For now, it's worth noting that earning money and receiving income (of whatever amount) positions us to start saving wisely and giving generously, the focus of today's study.

Let's now look at saving. Proverbs 13:11 highlights the power of regular saving: "Dishonest money dwindles away, but whoever gathers money little by little makes it grow." I learned the importance of this the hard way. During our early years of married life, Karen and I were on board with the importance of giving but were not so good at saving. This meant that we rarely had much margin. After a while we began to realize the wisdom of sensible saving—not the fear-based, materialistic hoarding that Jesus regularly spoke against, but making wise provision for the future.

There are a number of different purposes for

saving. These include saving for emergencies (sometimes called a boiler fund), saving for our needs and future opportunities, and saving so that we can give more away. Something of this balance between spending on ourselves and giving to others is highlighted in 1 Timothy 6. In verse 17, Paul warns those who are financially wealthy of the dangers of being arrogant or putting their hope in wealth, 'which is so uncertain,' before encouraging them to 'put their hope in God, who richly provides everything for our enjoyment.' Then, in the very next verse he emphasizes the need for generosity: "Command them to do good, to be rich in good deeds, and to be generous and willing to share. In this way they will lay up treasure for themselves as a firm foundation for the coming age, so that they may take hold of the life that is truly life" (1 Timothy 6:18–19). This may be the most important reason of all to save. If we don't have money, we can't give money!

So let's talk briefly about generous giving. There's an oft-used illustration concerning the two seas in Israel. In the north is the Sea of Galilee. It's a beautiful sea, filled with fish. In the south, there's the Dead Sea, filled with salt and chemicals where nothing of substance can live. The main difference between the two is that the Sea of Galilee has an inflow and an outflow, while the Dead Sea, the lowest place on Earth, has only an inflow and no outflow. It's the same with our lives. Generosity not only helps others but is a key to our own flourishing.

Research has shown that being generous helps contribute to our sense of wellness. There's something about being altruistic that activates a part of our brain that makes us feel happier. People who are more generous are generally happier, less depressed, and healthier—and this is something that the Bible has long taught. Jesus Himself famously stated, "It is more blessed to give than to receive" (Acts 20:35). But generosity doesn't just benefit our feelings, it also affects our finances! Contrary to what we might expect, the Bible teaches that because God is generous, when we're generous He is waiting to resupply us with His abundance. This is taught consistently throughout the Bible. For example, in Proverbs 11:24–25 we read: "One person gives freely, yet gains even more; another withholds unduly, but comes to poverty. A generous person will prosper; whoever refreshes others will be refreshed."

This is a stunning declaration of the link between generosity and financial thriving. Of course, the Bible doesn't teach that we should give to get; rather that we get to give. It's a privilege! Our motivation should be one of gratitude and a desire to be generous towards others. We're not supposed to give "reluctantly or under compulsion, for God loves a cheerful giver" (2 Corinthians 9:7). As we give generously with gratitude and joy, we have this promise: "God is able to bless you abundantly, so that in all things at all times, having all that you need, you will abound in every good work" (2 Corinthians 9:8). We can never out-give God!

REFLECT & RESPOND

Take some time to think about how you can save and give more. Maybe you need to revisit your spending and be more radical in cutting back. Then try to start saving regularly, even if it's only a small amount. Ask the Lord to help you to be ready to be generous whenever you can.

DAY 40

A journey of generosity

"It is more blessed to give than to receive."

ACTS 20:35

Yesterday we began to look at the link between generosity and thriving financially. While generosity can be spontaneous, my experience (and that of many others) is that if we want to weave generosity into the fabric of our lives, we need to do so with a measure of intentionality and planning. Indeed, in 1 Corinthians 16:23, Paul encourages his readers to build giving into the rhythm of their lives: "On the first day of every week, each one of you should set aside a sum of money in keeping with your income, saving it up, so that when I come no collections will have to be made." Notice here four things: giving is to be ***prioritized***; ***regular*** ("on the first day of every week"); ***planned*** ("set aside a sum of money"); and ***proportional*** ("in keeping with your income").

First, let's talk about giving as a ***priority***. Once again, we see this illustrated in the story of Elijah in 1 Kings 17. During the drought, God instructs His prophet to go to a widow in Zarephath. He arrives to find the widow preparing her last meal for herself and her son, before getting ready to die. If I was Elijah I might have said: "God, don't You have a better plan than this, like sending me to a wealthy family?" But Elijah didn't question God. Instead, he said to this destitute woman, "Don't be afraid ... first make a small loaf of bread for me from what you have and bring it to me, and then make something for yourself and your son" (1 Kings 17:13). Notice the order: *first* make something for me and then something for yourself. Was Elijah being self-serving or cruel? Neither—he was introducing this widow to the principle of putting God first, for her own good. Here was the promise: "The jar of flour will not be used up and the jug of oil will not run dry until the day the LORD sends rain on the land" (v. 14). And it happened just as God had promised: "There was food every day for Elijah and for the woman and her family" (v. 15). Although this is a unique story, the principle of giving *first* to God runs throughout the Bible. If we believe that God is the Lord of our lives, then He must be put first. Why? Because ultimately, He gave us the first and the very best, His firstborn Son, that we might be adopted into His family.

Second, let's talk about giving that is *regular, planned*, and *proportional*. Some consider that the starting place for this kind of giving is the long-established biblical principle of bringing a "tithe" (a tenth) of one's income as an act of worship to God (see Genesis 14:20; Leviticus 27:30; Malachi 3:10–11; Matthew 23:23). Others put the focus on the broader New Testament principle of grace-motivated generosity which we briefly touched on yesterday (see 2 Corinthians 8–9).

I started tithing as a relatively new Christian. Feeling overwhelmingly grateful to God for saving me, I began to put Him first in every area of my life—my decisions, schedule, and relationships. I then started hearing that tithing would honor God and help others. This seemed the right thing to do. When I got married, Karen and I continued to tithe as a starting point, and motivated by the desire to honor God and seeing it as a privilege to give, we have since increased our giving beyond this.

We've seen amazing provision in our lives as a result. On one occasion, many years ago, we needed a car. We didn't have the cash, and we'd agreed we weren't going to borrow, but we were still tithing, giving, and praying. Then, totally unexpectedly, someone came to us and offered us a car—a well-maintained red Ford Escort. That's just the first of countless stories of provision we've experienced over the years. We've also seen this principle at work in hundreds of church members, who can testify with us that honoring God with the first 10% and living off the other 90% is far better than trying to go it alone with 100%. Moreover, very often, once people start tithing and experience God's blessing, they are better positioned to give generously beyond this, not out of pressure but out of the joy of knowing God's grace at work in their lives.

REFLECT & RESPOND

However much or little you have, spend some time thanking God for His provision and invite Him to touch your heart with a fresh revelation of his love and generosity towards you. Look again at Paul's principles of giving that is prioritized, regular, planned, and proportional, and consider how you might take the next steps on your journey of generosity.

DAY 41

"Give us today our daily bread."

MATTHEW 6:11

Pray

One of the key moments in my own journey to live well financially was when I realized that not only was God interested in this area of my life, but He wanted me to pray about it.

With great joy, I discovered that praying for provision was embedded in the Lord's Prayer. Beginning with "Our Father, hallowed be Your name," I became aware that one of the covenant names of God was "Yahweh-Jireh" (Genesis 22:12), "the Lord who provides" (literally "the Lord who sees beforehand"). As I began to thank God and "hallow" His name every day, a deep confidence began to come over me that God would see to my every need. Then, having realigned my life by praying, "Your kingdom come, your will be done," I felt increasingly confident in praying, "Give us today our daily bread" (Matthew 6:11). I sought to pray this with these four principles in mind:

1. **Be in the will of God.** I realized that being in the will of God encompasses a lot of things. Broadly, it means living a lifestyle that's in alignment with His Word and following the

leading of His Spirit. In relation to my finances, that meant putting into practice the principles we've laid out so far, such as spending carefully, saving wisely, and giving generously. I realized that while God could and would supernaturally supply my needs, He also expected me to work diligently and honorably and that a key part of His provision would come to me in this way.

2. **Believe it's God's will to provide for you.** For me, this was about letting go of a poverty perspective and instead focusing on building my faith in God's goodness and His ability and willingness to provide. I spent some time reflecting on various biblical promises that relate to God's provision: "And my God will supply all your needs according to the riches of his glory in Christ Jesus" (Philippians 4:19); "And God is able to bless you abundantly, so that in all things at all times, having all that you need, you will abound in every good work" (2 Corinthians 9:8). Significantly, both these promises are in the context of generous giving. The result: "You will be enriched in every way so that you can be generous on every occasion, and through us your generosity will result in thanksgiving to God" (2 Corinthians 9:11). In other words, as we have seen over the last couple of days, when we give generously, God resupplies us so that we generously bless others and bring glory to Him.

3. **Be specific.** I remember how the Lord taught me and Karen to ask specifically for His provision. For a period of nine years, we kept a financial journal where we wrote down all that we gave in tithes and offerings and then wrote down our requests to God. We had such fun seeing God answer our specific requests—for ourselves, others, and the local church we had the privilege of leading.

4. **Be persistent.** Because we were so convinced that God wanted to provide for us in this way, we learned to become tenacious and not give up in our praying. I know Karen is particularly persistent when it comes to praying for other people's financial breakthroughs.

One of the best examples of someone praying this way is, of course, Elijah. In fact, the New Testament writer James uses Elijah's intercession for rain on behalf of the nation as a supreme example of faith-filled praying: "The prayer of a righteous person is powerful and effective. Elijah was a human being, even as we are. He prayed earnestly that it would not rain, and it did not rain on the land for three and a half years. Again, he prayed, and the heavens gave rain, and the earth produced its crops" (James 5:16–18). If we go back to the fuller account of the story in 1 Kings 18, we see how Elijah demonstrated all four of the principles outlined above. He was someone not just in the will of God but devoted to the will of God. He clearly believed that God would provide, boldly declaring to King Ahab that the rain would come. In this example he was not just praying for provision for himself but for a whole nation! He was also very specific in his asking, petitioning God for rain. Finally, his was an example of great persistence. Rather than being put off that his prayer was not immediately answered, he instructed his servant to go back seven times until he saw a cloud as small as a man's hand, a precursor to a heavy rainstorm (1 Kings 18:41–45).

There's much that we can learn from this great Old Testament man of faith and prayer, especially since we now have the greater privilege of praying, through Jesus to our heavenly Father: "Give us today our daily bread."

REFLECT & RESPOND

Have another look at the four principles of praying for provision that I've just outlined. Take a few moments to pray for specific needs, whether for yourself or for others.

DAY 42

"Keep your lives free from the love of money."

HEBREWS 13:5

God's school of finances

As we step back and summarize what we've looked at this week, I want you to imagine for a moment that God has a school with different levels of instruction where you can learn His principles of living well financially. (If you're not yet a Christian or are married to someone who isn't, you may not feel that all these principles can apply to you right now.)

The foundation class is entitled "Perspectives" and includes two key lessons:

- **Stewardship:** Here we learn that God is the owner and we are the stewards of everything that He has given us. Knowing this, we can make a fundamental decision to seek His guidance in managing our resources His way.
- **God's plan:** Here we discover that God has a plan for our financial health focused on Matthew 6:33, enabling us to get and stay free from a "poverty perspective" and a "materialistic mindset."

Once we have grasped these foundational perspectives, we can move on to the class entitled "Practices," which include three more lessons:

- **Spend carefully:** Here we appreciate the importance of learning contentment so that we can rein in our spending, with the goal of living within our means. As we do this, we get out of debt and begin to gain essential margin. This margin enables us to do two further things ...
- **Save wisely:** Without fear-based hoarding, we can set aside money for short-term emergencies and longer-term crises and opportunities.
- **Give generously:** This is the ultimate goal and one of the keys to us experiencing God's best in every area of our lives.

There is, however, an advanced class that the Lord may be calling you to attend. It's the "Surrender all to God" class. It's the most challenging of all, but it's also the most liberating, freeing us from the need to be in control, and trusting that ultimately God will take care of us.

This principle of surrendering to God is strikingly depicted in the calling of Elisha. Unlike the nomadic Elijah, it seems as if Elisha was relatively wealthy, plowing twelve yoke of oxen when first called by God. We read how:

> *"Elijah went up to him and threw his cloak around him. Elisha then left his oxen and ran after Elijah. 'Let me kiss my father and my mother goodbye,' he said, 'and then I will come with you.' 'Go back,' Elijah replied. 'What have I done to you?' So Elisha left him and went back. He took his yoke of oxen and slaughtered them. He burned the ploughing equipment to cook the meat and gave it to the people, and they ate. Then he set out to follow Elijah and became his servant" (1 Kings 19:19–21).*

The story of Elisha illustrates that there are times when the most important thing we can do is re-surrender all that we own to God. Sometimes this will require giving up literally everything to follow Him. This call to wholehearted service has many parallels in the story of Jesus' disciples leaving their nets to follow Him (see Matthew 4:19–20). So, is this a reckless thing to do? Not if we know it's the Lord calling us. In fact, we have this stunning promise from Jesus Himself: "Truly I tell you ... no one who has left home or brothers or sisters or mother or father or children or fields for me and the gospel will fail to receive a hundred times as much in this present age: homes, brothers, sisters, mothers, children and fields—along with persecutions—and in the age to come eternal life" (Mark 10:29–30). This promise of a hundred-fold return (including persecutions!) in this age, and eternal life in the age to come, is a staggering promise for all who will truly surrender everything to become His disciple. In other words, surrendering all to God—either literally (as in this case) or metaphorically (as a spiritual discipline)—is not only glorifying to Him but liberating for us.

REFLECT & RESPOND

Consider where you are on your journey of living well financially. What perspectives or practices do you need to attend to? What one thing do you want to focus on for the next month?

DAY 43

"For we are God's handiwork, created in Christ Jesus to do good works, which God prepared in advance for us to do."

EPHESIANS 2:10

Living on purpose

From the moment I accepted Jesus, I remember being filled not only with an overwhelming feeling of love, joy, and peace but also with a deep sense that I was born *on* purpose and *for* purpose. Not only has this general awareness of God's overall plan for me grown over many years of following Him, but so too has the clarity that I've enjoyed concerning His purpose for my life. Through years of experience, the help of the Holy Spirit, and the input of others, I can confidently articulate who it is that I am uniquely called to be, and what it is that I have specifically been called to do. This not only gives me fuel for forward movement but helps me know what to say no to, bringing an additional sense of focus and peace.

The Japanese have a word for this: *ikigai*, translated as "a reason for being" or "the reason for which you wake up in the morning." Being clear on our *ikigai* or life purpose is crucial for our wellbeing. Studies have shown that just as being purposeless increases the risk of depression, suicidal thoughts, poor social relationships, and substance and alcohol abuse, those with a stronger sense of purpose tend to act in ways that increase their physical and mental wellness.

Central to our life purpose is the concept of "calling" (from the Latin *vocare*, from which we get our word "vocation"). So how do we go about finding and fulfilling our calling? First, by recognizing that we have both an overall life purpose that is common to us all and a specific pathway that is unique to each one of us.

Let me illustrate. It's the 2004 Olympics in Athens, and the American rifle shooter Matt Emmons is one shot away from the gold medal. He aims his rifle at a target 50 meters away, takes a deep breath, and fires. He hits the bullseye! But the computer registers nothing. He shrugs, then calls over the judges. They shrug, too. Did the gun or the computer malfunction? Neither. Emmons had hit a target—but the wrong one! He dropped from first place to eighth, from a gold medal to no medal. This is a very poignant picture of what it's like if we miss our vocation in life. Finding our overall purpose is like hitting the right target, and discovering our unique pathway is like hitting the bullseye. Today, let's think about the target.

To find our overall life purpose, we need to look to the One who ultimately created us. This is at the heart of what Rick Warren explores in his best-selling book *The Purpose Driven Life*, in which he says this: "If you want to know why you were placed on this planet, you must begin with God. You were born by his purpose and for his purpose. ... Until you understand that, life will never make sense. It is only in God that we discover our origin, our identity, our meaning, our purpose, our significance, and our destiny. Every other path leads to a dead end."[1]

There have been various attempts at summarizing what the Bible reveals concerning our overall purpose. The seventeenth-century Westminster Confession famously taught that "the chief end of man is to glorify God and enjoy Him forever," adapted by John Piper to say "the chief end of man is to glorify God by enjoying Him forever."[2] In other words, our overall life purpose is strongly linked to matters of spiritual wellbeing that we explored earlier. Others have simply suggested that our overall purpose "is to know God and to make Him known."

Elijah was someone who lived with a healthy awareness of this overall God-centered purpose. As we saw back on Day 2, every time he heard his name "Eli-yah," "the LORD is my God," he was reminded that he owed his whole existence and identity to the Lord.

Likewise, with the very first words that we hear him declaring—"As the LORD, the God of Israel, lives, whom I serve ..." (1 Kings 17:1)—it's evident that he knew that his purpose came from being in relationship with and serving God.

This is not something unique to Elijah. In fact, knowing our God-given purpose and living it out is the birthright of every born-again child of God: "For we are God's handiwork, created in Christ Jesus to do good works, which God prepared in advance for us to do" (Ephesians 2:10).

REFLECT & RESPOND

Think about whether your vocational dial is on green, red, or yellow. Then consider whether you've been focusing your vocational energies on the wrong target, as this could be a key reason why you're not thriving. Think about how you might be able to make some changes to get back on track.

DAY 44

Following your pathway

"I praise you because I am fearfully and wonderfully made."

PSALM 139:14

Yesterday we saw that our vocation consists of two key elements. The first is to discover and live out our overall life purpose—which, in its simplest sense, is to know God and make Him known. The second, which we're focusing on today, is to find out and follow our specific life pathway.

A great example of this is Eric Liddell, the character at the center of the film *Chariots of Fire.*[3] An extremely gifted athlete and also a follower of Jesus, he knew that his overall purpose was about living for God. When in the 1924 Olympics it transpired that his favored event, the 100-meter sprint, was to be held on a Sunday, he courageously followed his personal conviction not to run. Instead, he went on to run in the 400 meters, a weekday event—and won the gold. Despite his incredible talent and Olympic potential, he felt that his ultimate calling was to serve the Lord as a missionary in China, and after two decades there, he died at the age of 43 in a Japanese civilian internment camp in 1945.

A great biblical example of someone who lived his life with the overall purpose of serving the Lord as well as fulfilling his specific calling was, of course, the prophet Elijah. Both before and after his burnout in 1 Kings 19, Elijah fulfilled his unique role as a national prophet, called to boldly declare God's will at a time of spiritual and moral decline. There were others, however, who still served God but in their own specific way. For example, there is the unnamed servant of Elijah, who was presumably called to support the prophet. There is also another interesting character in the story, a man called Obadiah. He also loved God but, unlike Elijah, stayed within the court, working very effectively from inside the system as the palace administrator—and in the process, he successfully hid and saved a hundred other prophets from Jezebel's murderous clutches (see 1 Kings 18:3–16). Both the servant and Obadiah played different but vital supporting roles. Each fulfilled their own unique calling without needing to become prophets. There is no sacred or secular division within the Bible, with those involved in "full-time" Christian ministry somehow more important than those who are fulfilling their calling in different ways—whether that be within the family, workplace, community, or local church.

This picture of the variety of specific gifts and callings is brought out more clearly in the New Testament. I remember many years ago studying various New Testament passages that contained lists of ministry gifts (notably Romans 12:3–6; 1 Corinthians 12:28; Ephesians 4:11–12) and was struck by how the more up-front roles of apostles, prophets, evangelists, pastors, and teachers were being celebrated in many contemporary church circles, while behind-the-scenes roles, such as the helpers, servers, and administrators were being undervalued. As I started teaching on and celebrating this gift of "helps" within the context of the local church, one couple suddenly felt empowered and liberated as they recognized that this wonderful calling was theirs.

Discovering our own unique calling might be a lifelong process, and over the years I have sought God for His clarity and confirmation as to my specific pathway. But there are also a number of different personality profiles that you may find really helpful, such as DISC, Myers-Briggs, Belbin, or Strength-Finder. What is important is to think as broadly as possible.

As you begin to think about your specific life purpose, here are a few final thoughts:

- Know that you are "fearfully and wonderfully made" (Psalm 139:14) and that you have a life pathway that is unique to you. Once again, let me encourage you not to fall into the comparison trap. Don't evaluate yourself by what you may consider to be other people's seemingly more glamorous or important callings. Your calling is the best one for you!
- Take a holistic approach that includes your work, studies, family life, and broader responsibility to serving your church or community.
- Recognize that finding your life purpose is almost always a journey of discovery that includes an ongoing process of extensive self-assessment and experimentation, consultation with others, and revelation from God.
- Understand that, like Eric Liddell, you may be fulfilling your vocation right now—but, as he discovered, you may have a different or perhaps even ultimate calling that lies somewhere else in the future.

REFLECT & RESPOND

As you begin to consider your unique pathway, why not start by asking these three questions:

- What can I do well? (Self-assessment and experimentation)
- What do others see in me? (Consultation)
- Is there an ultimate calling that I've not yet fulfilled? (Revelation)

DAY 45

In the flow

"Set your minds on things above, not on earthly things."

COLOSSIANS 3:2

When we live in the convergence of finding and fulfilling our overall life purpose and our specific life pathway, it's like hitting the correct target, right on the bullseye! We end up feeling alive, thinking things like, *I was born for this.* Eric Liddell, whose story we considered yesterday, famously talked of the joy he felt when he ran: "God made me fast. And when I run, I feel His pleasure." For me personally, the more I've sought to enjoy and please God in all things, and to discover the unique gifts and role that He's given me, the more fulfilled I've become—releasing me to bring my best for the good of others. I believe this is something God wants for all of us.

Many psychologists emphasize the importance of living out of our strengths. We're far more likely to flourish when we have the opportunity to act on our strengths and do what we do best. This is not to say that we live in a perfect world where we can spend all our time operating only in our areas of strength. Nevertheless, as we journey through life, we can seek ways either through paid work and/or other means of service to focus more of our time and attention on areas where we are strongest.

Studying the ministry life of Elijah, particularly the high point of 1 Kings 18, I've been struck many times by how he was able to accomplish remarkable things with seeming ease. His confidence in confronting and defeating the prophets of Baal, praying for rain, and outrunning the king's chariot are all a wonderful picture of someone living out of their God-given strengths.

Growing in clarity and confidence as to our unique strengths—and flourishing in them—helps us with a key area of wellbeing, which is the feeling of being "engaged." Engagement is linked to what psychologists call being in the "flow," where we feel our best and perform our best with total focus. Apparently, a "flow" experience causes a cascade of neurochemicals—adrenaline, dopamine, endorphins, anandamide, and oxytocin—to be released into our brain, causing us to have a natural high. Moreover, these experiences are performance enhancing: "Creativity has shown to increase 500–700% in a flow state. ... Flow has a documented correlation with high performance in the fields of artistic and scientific creativity, teaching, learning, and sports. ... It has been linked to persistence and achievement ... while also helping to lower anxiety during various activities and raise self-esteem."[4]

If we want to increase the amount of time we spend in a "flow" state, we need to think about how we are managing our energy (see Day 8). Since we only have a finite amount of energy daily—not just physically, but emotionally and creatively—it's important that we steward it well. Given that we all have various responsibilities to undertake each day, we need to recognize that we will perform better at certain times for certain tasks. The key to optimum performance is to recognize what those times and tasks are, and then give our best energy to the things that matter most. For example, I find that I'm the most alert physically and the most creative intellectually in the morning. In fact, very early in the morning! So for things that require the greatest energy and creativity, such as writing this book, I find I get so much more done if I get up and concentrate early on. Where possible I try and save other tasks, such as meetings and emails (which for me often require less creative energy) for later. I'm aware that you may be in a season of life in which you have less flexibility and perhaps have to focus a lot on responding to what others require of you. However, given the smaller margin that you are likely to have, it's even more important to use the little time and flexibility that you have to great effect.

The final issue I want to address today is the very practical matter of taking breaks. Our bodies, and especially our brains, were not designed to keep functioning optimally at the same level but rather, to function best in a series of "energy bursts" followed by time to rest and recover. Using breaks effectively is another key to increasing both our performance and our sense of wellness. Try viewing these as little gifts for your replenishment. I normally try to do some exercise in these breaks—even if only for a few minutes—and I nearly always include some brief time of prayer where I ask for fresh wisdom and strength. I then come back to the project or meeting feeling refreshed physically, emotionally, and spiritually, ready to give my best. It also means that I can enjoy increasing time "in the zone," which in turn has a massively positive impact on my ability to live well vocationally.

REFLECT & RESPOND

Consider times when you have been "in the flow"—what was it like? Did time stop for you? Were you completely absorbed in the task? Think about how you might be able to reorder your daily and weekly schedule to give your best time and energy to activities that matter the most.

DAY 46

"Go back the way you came."

1 KINGS 19:15

The need for perseverance

Even if we've discovered our life purpose and unique pathway and have experienced what it means to be "in the flow," it's still possible for us to lose our way. I'm sure all of us have experienced times when we've lost motivation, focus, and creativity. Sometimes, we may just want to quit. So if there's something else we need to live well vocationally, it's perseverance! The link between purpose and perseverance is clear. When we are passionate about something that is aligned with our purpose, we are more likely to persevere, make sacrifices, and stick to our course when problems arise.

One of the greatest examples of vocational perseverance is Abraham Lincoln. Born into poverty, Lincoln was faced with adversity throughout his life. He lost eight elections, failed twice in business, and suffered a nervous breakdown. He could have quit many times—but he didn't, and because he didn't give up, he is now considered to have been one of the greatest presidents in the history of the United States of America.

Sometimes we can feel so downhearted and discouraged that we need help to get back. We've already seen how Elijah displayed remarkable tenacity and perseverance in his early years of ministry. We've also noted how he came to the point of wanting to quit. In *The Message* version of the Bible, he's quoted as saying, "Enough of this, GOD! Take my life" (1 Kings 19:4). That's a pretty comprehensive resignation speech! But while Elijah may have been finished, God wasn't. Rather, having begun to revive him physically, emotionally, and spiritually, the Lord reaffirmed Elijah's calling with these simple but powerful words: "Go back the way you came" (1 Kings 19:15). It may well be that this call to go back the way he came was not just a reference to taking the same geographical route but was an encouragement for him to return to his original vocation. Having been replenished and having re-encountered the presence of God, he was ready to go back into the prophetic calling that he had nearly given up on. It may be that you, like Elijah, are thinking of giving up. You might need to reflect and reconsider if you simply need to "go back the way you came."

While our calling may stay the same, the way that we live it out may well change. As we have already seen (and will explore again tomorrow), Elijah went back the way he came but with a new assignment. First, God instructed him to go and anoint two new kings, which, sadly, the normally obedient prophet failed to do. Thankfully, he had a second assignment, which was to appoint Elisha to succeed him as prophet. This he did faithfully. So instead of quitting at a premature finish line, Elijah did get up, he did go back, and he persevered for a final ten years.

I don't know about you, but I've had times when I felt like quitting. Foremost of these was when we were first starting KingsGate Community Church. We were under pressure on all fronts—physically, emotionally, spiritually, relationally, and financially. Vocationally, I was feeling super stretched: working a new full-time teaching job, helping Karen as much as I could with looking after our young family, finishing a doctoral thesis, and toughest of all, trying to get the church established. After 18 months, the church had grown from nine to fifteen people, only for us to have a "backdoor revival" which left us six people, three of whom were our family. I was ready to quit and on a couple of occasions handed my resignation in to the Lord. I remember saying to Him, "I can't build this church," and, sensing the Lord smile, I heard Him say in return, "Good, I'm glad we've got that sorted!" (Jesus said, "I will build my church"—Matthew 16:18.) So

I began to get refocused in that season, with a growing awareness that if anything was going to happen it would be with the Lord working in and through me, not by my trying to get things done in my own strength. I also began to learn something of the power of perseverance.

Wherever you're at today, especially if you're in or heading towards the vocational red zone and are contemplating giving up, I encourage you: don't quit. Don't stop at a false line. Keep on going until the end.

REFLECT & RESPOND

Maybe you are struggling with a loss of motivation, creativity, or energy, or even wanting to quit. Maybe you just need an increase in clarity and confidence concerning your vocation. Wherever you're at, take time to reflect. Are there steps you can take to reignite your sense of calling and destiny? Re-embrace your purpose and determine to persevere—right to the end!

DAY 47

Alone or with other people

"As iron sharpens iron, so one person sharpens another."

PROVERBS 27:17

There are two ways in which we can try to fulfill our calling: alone or with other people. As we've seen already, having friends and functioning in community is vital for living well relationally, strengthening and protecting us and those we're in relationship with. Today we're going to focus on the huge vocational benefits brought by working with others.

One author summarizes it this way: "The undeniable reality is that how well you do in life and in business depends not only on what you do and how you do it, your skills and competencies, but also on who is doing it with you or to you. ... When you get the power of the other on your side, you can surpass whatever limit you are currently experiencing or will ever experience in the future."[5] In other words, when we have others alongside us, we're no longer limited to just our gifts but have the compounded benefits of partnership and teamwork of differently gifted people. Furthermore, working together with others of various ages means that our influence is multiplied and accessible to different generations.

For the first part of his ministry, Elijah operated

largely as a lone ranger, a model that left him isolated and very vulnerable. It also meant that if he'd died in the desert as he requested, his prophetic ministry would have died with him. Thankfully, his encounter with the Lord on Mount Horeb proved to be a turning point. As he went back into the final phase of his ministry, he was no longer a lone prophet but had a young friend and successor working alongside him. In fact, it seems that he spent the next ten years mentoring Elisha. There's no suggestion that Elijah was perfect—we know he wasn't—yet his life had such an impact on Elisha that the younger man's final request before they parted was for "a double portion of your spirit" (2 Kings 2:9).

This call to work with and mentor others is not something that was unique to Elijah. Jesus supremely modeled this by spending the best part of three and half years with His twelve disciples. Then, before He left the earth to go to heaven, He gave them and the fledgling church the Great Commission: to "go and make disciples" (Matthew 28:19). The apostle Paul picks up on this theme with a young man, Timothy: "You then, my son, be strong in the grace that is in Christ Jesus. And the things you have heard me say in the presence of many witnesses entrust to reliable people who will also be qualified to teach others" (2 Timothy 2:1–2).

This emphasis on life-on-life discipling and the longevity of these relationships—ten years for Elijah and Elisha, just over three years for Jesus and His disciples—highlights that commitment is needed from both parties.

There's a broader principle I want to conclude with, which concerns the power of teamwork. To quote a slightly corny but largely true statement: "Teamwork makes the dream work." Personally, I've found that the more I've discovered who I am, the more I've discovered who I'm not. The more I realize what I'm good at, the more I realize what I'm not good at. I'm now hugely appreciative of being part of great teams of differently gifted men and women and am so aware of the synergy and multiplying effect of working with others.

As you step back and reflect, take time to consider whether you need to make changes to the way you are operating either in your work or wider service. Are you functioning as a lone ranger or are you already working with others? Either way, think about how you can increase your investment in other people and grow in functioning within the context of teams.

DAY 48

"You will receive power when the Holy Spirit comes on you."

ACTS 1:8

The power of the Spirit

As a church leader, part of my job is teaching on Sundays at KingsGate Peterborough—an auditorium that currently seats 1,500 people. If I tried to speak in that relatively large space using just the strength of my own voice, I would struggle to project very far. However, with the right level of amplification, I can communicate clearly and with a lot less effort. Today we're going to look at how God has given us something (or, more accurately, someone) who acts as an amplifier to our gifts: the Holy Spirit.

Throughout the Bible, we see the Holy Spirit filling people to amplify their gifts and to empower them to fulfill their God-given purpose, such as Bezalel for artistic work (Exodus 31:2–5), Gideon for leadership (Judges 6:15, 34), and Samson for strength (Judges 15:14). It was the same Holy Spirit who was the power behind Elijah's ministry. This helps answer the question as to how someone who was "a human being, even as we are" (James 5:17) could speak the revelatory words and perform the mighty miracles that he did. It's not just that he was a great man of faith and prayer, he had the power of the Spirit working with and through him.

The work of the Spirit in Elijah's life is evident: implicit throughout his early ministry years, and then specifically referred to in 1 Kings 18:46, when "the power of the LORD came on Elijah" and he outran the king's chariot. Later, just prior to his being taken up to heaven, we see the Spirit's power through the imagery of Elijah's cloak. He and Elisha were at the Jordan River when "Elijah took his cloak, rolled it up and struck the water with it. The water divided to the right and to the left, and the two of them crossed over on dry ground" (2 Kings 2:8). This is clearly more than the physical act of a piece of fabric parting the river! Rather, it represented his prophetic gift that came not from himself, but from the Holy Spirit. Immediately after this, Elisha makes one final request: "Let me inherit a double portion of your spirit" (2 Kings 2:9). In other words, Elisha recognizes that Elijah is operating not just with natural strength but with spiritual power. After Elisha has seen Elijah taken up to heaven, we read this in 2 Kings 2:13–15:

> *"Elisha then picked up Elijah's cloak that had fallen from him and went back and stood on the bank of the Jordan. He took the cloak that had fallen from Elijah and struck the water with it. "Where now is the LORD, the God of Elijah?" he asked. When he struck the water, it divided to the right and to the left, and he crossed over. The company of the prophets from Jericho, who were watching, said, 'The spirit of Elijah is resting on Elisha.'"*

The cloak was symbolic of the power of the Spirit of God, which had rested on Elijah's life. Elisha knew that this was the key and so asked for a double portion of this power. He asked, received, and went on to do even greater miracles than his master.

So, how does all of this apply to us? In a wonderful parallel New Testament passage, Luke records how Jesus—like Elijah but far greater than Elijah—was getting ready to ascend to heaven. Before going, He prepared his Elisha-like disciples and promised them that the same Holy Spirit that had anointed Him would be poured out on them: "You are witnesses of these things. I am going to send you what my Father has promised; but stay in the city until you have been clothed with power from on high" (Luke 24:48–49). The parallel with Elijah and Elisha is striking. Jesus was saying something of huge importance. The Church is called to continue His overall purpose of knowing Him and making Him known and for that, we need to be clothed with the same Holy Spirit as Jesus was. This power was poured out on the waiting disciples on the day of Pentecost and is still available to the Church today (see Luke 11:13; Acts 2:1–4; 2:38–39).

Just as Elijah was anointed to be a prophet, so we can be anointed for our vocation, too—whether that be within our families, place of work, local church, or within our community.

REFLECT & RESPOND

As you reflect on the wonderful promise of the Holy Spirit, consider whether you have received this great gift. If not, why not ask God to fill you with His power in order to help you be more effective in your vocation or specific life calling?

DAY 49

"Whatever you do, work at it with all your heart."

COLOSSIANS 3:23

Promise of rewards

What do you do when work feels like a grind? Maybe you're operating in a situation that is less than ideal and it's just tough. Do you find yourself wondering whether what you're doing is worthwhile? Even if right now you're in a season where you're grateful to be spending much of your time living and working in your vocational sweet spot, it doesn't mean that what you're doing won't sometimes seem tough, even boring! So how do we keep going? How do we maintain vocational motivation when we don't feel particularly fired up?

For those of us who are Christians, the answer is by living our whole lives in gratitude to the God who has called us, knowing that ultimately He will reward us. Paul summarizes it this way: "And whatever you do, whether in word or deed, do it all in the name of the Lord Jesus, giving thanks to God the Father through him" (Colossians 3:17). The "whatever you do" is deliberately set in the broader context of a passage that has been talking about life and relationships within the Church and is immediately followed by a section focusing on relationships in the family, at work, and in the community. In other words, our overall life purpose is to know God and make Him known in every sphere of our lives—whether we're working full time, studying, looking after children or elderly parents, retired, or doing voluntary work. Then Paul gives us an ultimate motivation for living this way. A few verses later, he repeats the same phrase, this time emphasizing the matter of rewards: "Whatever you do, work at it with all your heart ... since you know that you will receive an inheritance from the Lord as a reward. It is the Lord Christ you are serving" (Colossians 3:23–24). The simple but profound truth is that for all of us, in whatever sphere we're functioning, everything we do is to be for the Lord. We live and work with an eternal perspective: since this life is not the end, and there is life after life, when Jesus comes back there will be rewards in the age to come.

We don't know what reward Elijah will get when Christ returns, but it does seem that God was pleased with his faithful (though not perfect) service. First, he had a great send-off! Rather than die, he was accompanied up to heaven in a whirlwind by a chariot of fire. Second the prophet Malachi spoke of the importance of Elijah's ministry and his returning before the Day of the Lord—calling for repentance, reconciliation, and changed hearts, particularly in families (Malachi 4). Third, Elijah, along with Moses, reappeared on earth at one of the high points of Jesus' ministry on the Mount of Transfiguration (see Matthew 17:1–4). We don't know what they talked about, but Jeff Lucas has suggested the following: "Is it possible that, as Jesus faced the final great step of obedience, Elijah, who did wonderfully but stopped short of God's total best, encourages his Lord to go the whole way, pay the final price, be the ultimate radical? Perhaps one day we will know. What we do know is that this ordinary man, who was 'just like us' was given an encore of honor during Transfiguration moments."[6]

While none of us will experience quite such an encore as Elijah had, if we put our trust in God, we have the promise that we will receive a reward for faithful (if sometimes faltering) service. We don't get everything we desire in this life, and our work can be tough in this imperfect world. However, as we live life well and stay true to our God-given vocation, we are storing up great rewards in the age to come. Then, together with Elijah and multitudes of others, we'll hear the voice of the Lord Himself saying, "Well done—come and enjoy my complete and perfect *shalom* forever!"

REFLECT & RESPOND

Think about the kind of impact you would like to make and what kind of legacy you would like to leave behind. Then think about the promise of eternal rewards. Consider how you may want to make changes to your approach to your life, ministry, and work. Receive fresh strength and motivation in "whatever you do."

EVER-INCREASING WELLBEING

DAY 50

"The LORD be exalted, who delights in the well-being of his servant."

PSALM 35:27

Thriving more each day

The message of this book has been that God really does have a plan for you to live well in every area of your life—physically, emotionally, spiritually, relationally, financially, and vocationally. As we come to this final day, I hope that you'll view this not so much as the end of a 50-day guide, but as an invitation to a lifetime journey of living well!

In a classically Christmas Bible passage that heavily influenced Handel's *Messiah*, God revealed His long-established plan for our thriving, centered on the coming of the Messiah: "For to us a child is born, to us a son is given; and the government shall be upon his shoulder, and his name shall be called Wonderful Counsellor, Mighty God, Everlasting Father, Prince of Peace [*shalom*]. Of the increase of his government and of peace [*shalom*] there will be no end" (Isaiah 9:6–7 ESV). This was fulfilled when Jesus came not just to bring peace and thriving, but as the very source of our peace and thriving. So God not only has a plan, but through Jesus and by His Holy Spirit, He has personally come so that you and I can experience His best in every area of our lives.

However, if we want to enjoy these benefits, we need to be prepared to do some of the work—and make sure we introduce rhythms that line up with God's perfect plan.

We start by **submitting to His plan for our lives**. Before we can experience an increase of His peace, we need an increase of His government or rulership in our lives. If you haven't yet made Jesus the Lord of your life, I strongly encourage you to do so! It will be the best decision you'll ever make. If you are already a follower of Christ, then make a fresh commitment to put Him first.

Next, we need to **keep renewing our minds in line with His truth**. As we have learned, if we are going to live well, we need to start by developing a mindset for living well.

In order to keep moving forward, we need to **continue being intentional in taking our next steps**. I trust you've already made some positive progress and taken some significant steps forward over the past 50 days. What's important is that you don't stop now!

Next, we **make ourselves accountable**. This might seem a little vulnerable or even uncomfortable at first, but we are far more likely to keep making progress if we write down next steps, share them with other people, and then invite them to regularly ask how we are doing. Let's celebrate the little wins! And whatever happens, let's keep going. Don't be discouraged if, for example, you don't see immediate results. We rarely do. But as you keep on going, little by little you'll notice a difference.

Finally, **give it away.** The ultimate purpose of your thriving is not just for your good but for others, too. God is concerned for our wellbeing but He is also passionate about the wellbeing of the communities, cities, and nation that we're a part of. In a compelling letter sent by Jeremiah to the exiles in Babylon, the Lord urged His people: "Seek peace and well-being for the city where I have sent you into exile, and pray to the LORD on its behalf; for in its peace (well-being) you will have peace" (Jeremiah 29:7 AMP).

My prayer is that each of us will live well and thrive, and that our wellbeing will overflow to everyone around us, in the name of Jesus, the Prince of Wellbeing!

REFLECT & RESPOND

Consider again each of the six areas of your life that we've covered over the past 50 days. Review any notes you have made and, for each area, reflect on the one thing you think will have the greatest impact as you move forward. Make sure that you're as specific as possible. The point is not just to have noble aspirations but achievable next steps.

A Prayer of Invitation

Lord Jesus, I admit my need of You and invite You to come and forgive me. I believe that You died and rose again so that I could receive new joy, purpose, hope, and wellbeing. Please come into my life and fill me with Your Holy Spirit. I commit to follow You and Your ways all the days of my life. Amen!

I affirm that in Christ . . .

I am eternally loved by God. (Jeremiah 31:3; Ephesians 1:5)

I am personally chosen by God. (Ephesians 1:4; John 15:16)

I am saved by God's amazing grace. (Ephesians 2:8–9)

I am adopted into God's family. (Romans 8:15–17; Ephesians 1:5)

I am completely forgiven. (Colossians 1:13–14; Ephesians 1:7–8)

I am the righteousness of God. (Romans 5:17; 2 Corinthians 5:21)

I am a new creation. (2 Corinthians 5:17)

I am God's masterpiece. (Ephesians 2:10)

I am being sanctified. (Romans 6:1–14)

I belong to God. (Romans 14:7–8; 1 Peter 2:9)

I am the dwelling place of God. (1 Corinthians 3:16; Galatians 2:20)

I am God's heir and a co-heir with Christ. (Romans 8:16–17)

I am deeply and unconditionally loved by God. (Romans 8:38–39; Ephesians 3:18–19)

Endnotes

Introduction

[1] See "What is Well-Being?," posted 2 January 2019 on psychologytoday.com [accessed August 2020]

[2] Statistics taken from Stress in America 2023 by the American Psychological Association. An overview can be found at: apa.org/news/press/releases/stress/2023/collective-trauma-recovery [accessed January 2024]

[3] Luke McKenna, *Making Wellbeing Practical* (Australia: Publicious, 2019), 7.

[4] For a more in-depth, and broader biblical treatment of this whole topic see, *The Bible and Mental Health*, ed. Christopher C.H. Cook and Isabelle Hamley, SCM Press, 2020).

Days 1–7: A Mindset to Live Well

[1] Selwyn Hughes, *Christ Empowered Living* (Farnham: CWR, 2005), 232–234.

[2] Statements taken from the National Institute of Mental Health website: nimh.nih.gov/health/topics/caring-for-your-mental-health [accessed January 2024]

[3] Walt Disney Pictures: *The Lion King* (1994)

[4] One of the summaries of our new identity in Christ is found in the early chapters of Paul's letter to the Ephesians. I have written extensively on this in my book *Transformed Life* (Farnham: CWR, 2015).

[5] Story taken from preceptaustin.org/christ_our_rock [accessed August 2020]

[6] Neil T. Anderson, *Living Free in Christ* (Ventura, CA, USA: Regal Books/Monarch, 1993), 94–97.

[7] Henry Cloud gave an online webinar on "The Psychology of Crisis" on 25 March 2020

[8] Ruth Haley Barton, *Invitation to Solitude and Silence* (Downers Grove, IL, USA: IVP, 2010), 58–59.

[9] Based on Henry Cloud's message on "Reversing the Death Spiral of a Leader," given in Session 3 of the Global Leadership Summit in 2013

[10] Taken from Nick Vujkicic's YouTube channel (Youtube.com/user/NickVujicicTV) [accessed August 2020]

[11] Carol Dweck, *Mindset: Changing the Way You Think to Fulfil Your Potential* (London: Robinson, 2017)

[12] Luke McKenna, *Making Wellbeing Practical*, 114.

Days 8–14: Live Well Physically

[1] There are various adaptions of Maslow's theory out there, but I recommend a quick Google of the pyramid if it helps you to visualize.

[2] Jim Loehr and Tony Schwartz, *The Power of Full Engagement* (New York: Free Press, 2015), 48.

[3] George Whitefield, *George Whitefield's Journals* (Edinburgh: Banner of Truth Trust, 1978), 441.

[4] Ruth Haley Barton, *Invitation*, 56.

[5] Statistics taken from the Mental Health Foundation website: mentalhealth.org.uk [accessed August 2020]. For further reading on this subject, I recommend the article "Sleep Matters: The Impact of Sleep On Health and Wellbeing," found at bupa.co.uk/newsroom [accessed August 2020]

[6] Based on Matthew Walker, *Why We Sleep* (London: Penguin Random House, 2017), 341–342.

[7] John J. Ratey, Spark: *The Revolutionary New Science of Exercise and the Brain* (London: Quercus, 2009), 4.

[8] Charles Duhigg, *The Power of Habit* (London: Random House, 2013), cited in Luke McKenna, *Making Wellbeing Practical*, 142–143.

[9] James Clear, *Atomic Habits: An Easy and Proven Way to Build Good Habits and Break Bad Ones* (New York: Penguin Random House USA, 2018), 15.

Days 15–21: Live Well Emotionally

[1] There are a number of different personality tests out there, but there are lots of resources available that teach these very helpful principles with a Christian worldview and within a sound biblical framework. The idea is not to box people in but help us identify and understand the gifts and strengths that God has given us. They are usually highly affirming and helpful for team building, as well as for personal introspection and discipleship.

[2] Peter Scazzero, *The Emotionally Healthy Leader* (Grand Rapids, MI, USA: Zondervan, 2015)

[3] Barbara Fredrickson, *Positivity* (London: One World, 2011), 33.

[4] Barbara Fredrickson, *Positivity*, 32.

[5] Larry Warner, *Journey with Jesus: Discovering the Spiritual Exercises of Saint Ignatius* (London: IVP Books UK, 2010)

[6] Viktor Frankl, *Man's Search for Meaning* (originally published 1946)

[7] Barbara Fredrickson, *Positivity*, 41.

[8] Robert Emmons, *Thanks! How the new science of gratitude can make you happier* (New York: Houghton Mifflin, 2007), cited in Luke McKenna, *Making Wellbeing Practical*, 46.

[9] Martin Seligman, *Flourish* (Great Britain: Nicolas Brealey Publishing, 2011), 30–35.

[10] John Mark Comer, *The Ruthless Elimination of Hurry* (London: Hodder and Stoughton, 2019), 18–19.

[11] Dan Allender, *Sabbath* (Nashville, TN, USA: Thomas Nelson, 2009), cited in John Mark Comer, *The Ruthless Elimination of Hurry*, 135.

[12] John Mark Comer, *The Ruthless Elimination of Hurry*, 148–149.

[13] Walter Brueggemann, *Sabbath as Resistance: Saying No to the Culture of Now* (Louisville, KY, USA: Westminster John Knox Press, 2014), cited in John Mark Comer, *The Ruthless Elimination of Hurry*, 130.

Days 22–28: Live Well Spiritually

[1] Selwyn Hughes, *Christ Empowered Living*, 107.

[2] Ruth Haley Barton, *Invitation to Silence and Solitude*, 51.

[3] Henri Nouwen, *Spiritual Direction: Wisdom for the Long Walk of Faith* (New York, HarperOne, 2006), cited in John Mark Comer, *The Ruthless Elimination of Hurry*, 135.

[4] Jeff Lucas, *Faith For All Seasons* (Farnham: CWR, 2016) 143.

[5] Nicky Gumbel, *Questions of Life* (Eastbourne: Kingsway, 1993) 95.

[6] For more on how to pray the Lord's Prayer, you can find some helpful information at transformedlife.co.uk or read Pete Greig's *How to Pray* (London: Hodder and Stoughton, 2019)

[7] The Church of England's "Daily Prayer" app is available to download for free from your smartphone app provider and is a great way to daily engage in prayer alongside countless others around the world

[8] From *Soul Nourishment First*, a booklet by George Müller, 9 May 1841

[9] "SOAP" principles based on the ideas of Wayne Cordeiro, *The Divine Mentor* (Bloomington, MN, USA: Bethany House Publishers, 2008)

[10] Pope Benedict XVI, Sunday Angelus, 6 November 2005

[11] Larry Warner, *Discernment, God's Will & Living Jesus* (barefooted publishing, 2016) 90.

[12] John Mark Comer, *The Ruthless Elimination of Hurry,* 133.

[13] Larry Warner, *Discernment*, 90.

[14] Jeff Lucas, *Faith For All Seasons*, 150.

[15] If you want to develop this practice more fully, I recommend reading Ruth Haley Barton's *Invitation to Solitude and Silence.*

Days 29–35: Live Well Relationally

[1] E. Diener and M. Seligman, "Very Happy People," *Psychological Science* (2002), cited in Luke McKenna, *Making Wellbeing Practical*, 75.

[2] Luke McKenna, *Making Wellbeing Practical*, 75–76.

[3] Holt-Lunstad, 2010; 2015

[4] Henry Cloud, *The Power of the Other* (Harper Business, Kindle ed. 2013), Chapter Three: "The Four Corners of Connection"

[5] Jeff Lucas, *Faith For All Seasons*, 128.

[6] Based on Edward Hall's extensive research on Proxemics

[7] Rick Warren, *The Purpose Driven Life* (Grand Rapids, MI, USA: Zondervan, 2002) 121, 130.

[8] John Townsend, *People Fuel: Fill Your Tank for Life, Love and Leadership* (Grand Rapids, MI, USA: Zondervan, 2019) 209.

[9] John Townsend, *People Fuel,* 41.

[10] John Townsend, *People Fuel*, 53–54.

[11] For more on this important subject see, Dr. Henry Cloud and Dr. John Townsend, *Boundaries,* (Grand Rapids, MI, USA: Zondervan, 1992, 2017).

[12] The Marriage Course is a wonderful resource for exploring foundational, biblical principles for lasting marriages in a relaxed and accessible way. Find out more at themarriagecourse.org.

[13] I recommend Gary Chapman, *The 5 Love Languages* (Chicago, IL, USA: Northfield Publishing, 1995) for exploring this further. The basic premise is that each of us has a primary "love language" by which we give and receive love: acts of service, thoughtful gifts, physical touch, quality time, or words of affirmation. You can begin identifying yours online at 5lovelanguages.com.

[14] Based on overall concepts of John Townsend's *People Fuel*, Part 2: "The Nutrients"

[15] Rick Warren, *The Purpose Driven Life*, 127.

[16] Sometimes the wounds of offense can be so deep that you may need to get help from a wise pastoral leader or counselor.

[17] For more about the Alpha Course visit www.alpha.org.

[18] Dave Smith, *Living the Dream* (Farnham: CWR, 2016)

Days 36–42: Live Well Financially

[1] Statistics taken from the Stress In America 2023 Survey. https://www.apa.org/news/press/releases/stress/2023/collective-trauma-recovery [Accessed January 2024]

[2] Citizens Advice Bureau: www.citizensadvice.org.uk; Christians Against Poverty: www.capuk.org; Community Money Advice: www.communitymoneyadvice.com

Days 43–49: Live Well Vocationally

[1] Rick Warren, *The Purpose Driven Life*, 17–18.

[2] John Piper, *Desiring God: Meditations of a Christian Hedonist* (Portland, OR, USA: Multnomah Press, 2011)

[3] Warner Bros: *Chariots of Fire* (1981)

[4] Luke McKenna, *Making Wellbeing Practical*, 62.

[5] See Henry Cloud, *The Power of the Other*, Chapter 1: "The Neglected Truth"

[6] Jeff Lucas, *Faith For All Seasons*, 190.

Bibliography

Allender, Dan, *Sabbath* (Nashville, TN, USA: Thomas Nelson, 2009)

Anderson, Neil T., *Living Free in Christ* (Ventura, CA, USA: Regal Books/Monarch, 1993)

Brueggemann, Walter, *Sabbath as Resistance:* (Louisville, KY, USA: Westminster John Knox Press, 2014)

Cacioppo, John, and Patrick, William, *Loneliness* (New York: Norton, 2008)

Chapman, Gary, *The Five Love Languages* (Chicago, IL, USA: Northfield Publishing, 1995)

Clear, James, *Atomic Habits* (New York: Penguin Random House USA, 2018)

Dr. Cloud, Henry and Townsend, John, *Boundaries* (Grand Rapids, MI, USA: Zondervan, 1992, 2017)

Cloud, Henry, *The Power of the Other* (London: HarperCollins, 2016)

Cook, Christopher C.H. and Hamley, Isabelle, *The Bible and Mental Health*, ed. (London: SCM Press, 2020)

Comer, John Mark, *The Ruthless Elimination of Hurry* (London: Hodder and Stoughton, 2019)

Cordeiro, Wayne, *The Divine Mentor* (Bloomington, MN, USA: Bethany House Publishers, 2008)

Duhigg, Charles, *The Power of Habit* (London: Random House, 2013)

Dweck, Carol, *Mindset* (London: Robinson, 2017)

Emmons, Robert, *Thanks!* (New York: Houghton Mifflin, 2007)

Frankl, Viktor, *Man's Search for Meaning* (originally published 1946)

Fredrickson, Barbara, *Positivity* (London: One World, 2011)

Greig, Pete, *How to Pray* (London: Hodder and Stoughton, 2019)

Gumbel, Nicky, *Questions of Life* (Eastbourne: Kingsway, 1993)

Haley Barton, Ruth, *Invitation to Solitude and Silence* (Downers Grove, IL, USA: IVP, 2010)

Hughes, Selwyn, *Christ Empowered Living* (Farnham: CWR, 2005)

Loehr, Jim, and Schwartz, Tony, *The Power of Full Engagement* (New York: Free Press, 2015)

Lucas, Jeff, *Faith For All Seasons* (Farnham: CWR, 2016)

McKenna, Luke, *Making Wellbeing Practical* (Australia: Publicious, 2019)

Nouwen, Henri, *Spiritual Direction* (New York: HarperOne, 2006)

Piper, John, *Desiring God* (Portland, OR, USA: Multnomah Press, 2011)

Ratey, John J., *Spark* (London: Quercus, 2009)

Scazzero, Pete, *The Emotionally Healthy Leader* (Grand Rapids, MI, USA: Zondervan, 2015)

Seligman, Martin, *Authentic Happiness* (New York: Free Press, 2002)

Seligman, Martin, *Flourish* (Great Britain: Nicolas Brealey Publishing, 2011)

Smith, Dave, *Living the Dream* (Farnham: CWR, 2016)

Townsend, John, *People Fuel* (Grand Rapids, MI, USA: Zondervan, 2019)

Walker, Matthew, *Why We Sleep* (London: Penguin Random House, 2017)

Warner, Larry, *Journey with Jesus* (London: IVP Books UK, 2010)

Warner, Larry, *Discernment, God's Will & Living Jesus* (barefooted publishing, 2016)

Warren, Rick, *The Purpose Driven Life* (Grand Rapids, MI, USA: Zondervan, 2002)

Whitefield, George, *George Whitefield's Journals* (Edinburgh: Banner of Truth Trust, 1978)

About the Author

DR. DAVE SMITH

Dave became a Christian while studying at Oxford University, where he went on to complete a doctorate in church history. He and his wife, Karen, moved to Peterborough in 1988 to start KingsGate Community Church—now a large, multicultural, intergenerational, multisite church. Dave has a heart to see a revival of healthy believers and churches who in turn impact their neighbourhoods and the nations! He loves walking and is an avid Manchester City fan!